12 STEPS TO LOVING YOURSELF

12 Steps to Loving Yourself

Loving Your Enemy and Liking It

Dorothy Marie England

FORWARD MOVEMENT PUBLICATIONS
CINCINNATI, OHIO

Copyright 2002

Forward Movement Publications

412 Sycamore Street
Cincinnati, Ohio 45202
800-543-1813
www.forwardmovement.org

About the Author

Dorothy Marie England is a pseudonym used to respect A.A.'s tradition of anonymity. The author is a Licensed Clinical Social Worker and Certified Addiction Counselor who has been practicing for over 25 years. She is director of a regional mental health center's substance abuse programs, and has gained national recognition through numerous publications, including six articles in The Counselor Magazine, the publication of the National Association of Alcohol and Drug Abuse Counselors. A recovering alcoholic and drug addict with many years in the program of Alcoholics Anonymous, Ms. England is recently widowed. She is a mother and grandmother.

Ms. England's first husband was alcoholic, and ultimately died from alcohol-related causes. This generational, genetic disease of chemical dependency continues to plague family members. This book is not about alcoholism; it is about freedom, happiness and hope. Ms. England's pilgrimage through pain, confusion and despair to peace and joy reveals that *all* problems are spiritual. Only a spiritual path leads to the "peace the world cannot give." Here she explains how the Twelve Steps of A.A. will work for anyone willing to make this journey.

The book contains stories about Ms. England and people she has known. The problems of chemically dependent persons are no different from those of others; they aren't the only people victimized by anger, depression, fear and self-pity. These are common experiences. The Twelve Steps offer "a new freedom and a new happiness" to anyone and everyone willing to embrace this program of spiritual growth.

Contents

Dedicated to the memory of
The Rev. David C. Streett
Veteran of the U.S. Navy, World War II
Episcopal Priest
Recovering Alcoholic
and this book's first editor
without whom it would never have
seen the light of day

Foreword

Most of my life I was my own worst enemy. I did what I didn't want to do, said what I didn't want to say, and found myself where I didn't want to be with people who didn't seem to want me around.

I was tired, depressed, afraid, angry and resentful. I felt abused, unloved, worthless and useless. No matter how hard I tried to help others they didn't seem to care about me.

Now I do what I want to do, say what I want to say, and am always where I want to be with people I like. I'm energetic, joyful, peaceful and happy. I feel loved, worthwhile and powerful. People, even my family, are interested in what I have to say.

This all came about as the result of a simple program I began as a patient in a state mental hospital's chemical dependency treatment unit.

Through this program I learned to love myself, to love my neighbor, to love my family, and even to love my enemies. Also, I learned not to be my own enemy, and by doing so became no one else's enemy. Would you like to know this profound secret? It goes like this:

God, grant me the serenity to accept the things I cannot change, the courage to change the things I can, and the wisdom to know the difference.

—from a prayer by Reinhold Neibuhr

The Promises

If we are painstaking about this phase of our development, we will be amazed before we are halfway through. We are going to know a new freedom and a new happiness. We will not regret the past nor wish to shut the door on it. We will comprehend the word serenity and we will know peace. No matter how far down the scale we have gone, we will see how our experience can benefit others. The feeling of uselessness and self-pity will disappear. We will lose interest in selfish things and gain interest in our fellows. Self-seeking will slip away. Our whole attitude and outlook upon life will change. Fear of people and of economic insecurity will leave us. We will intuitively know how to handle situations which used to baffle us. We will suddenly realize that God is doing for us what we could not do for ourselves.

Are these extravagant promises? We think not. They are being fulfilled among us—sometimes quickly, sometimes slowly. They will always materialize if we work for them (Alcoholics Anonymous, A.A. World Services, Inc. Box 459, Grand Central Station, N.Y., N.Y. 10163, 1976, p.83-84).

These words are from the book which is the cornerstone of the Alcoholics Anonymous program, written by its co-founder Bill W. in 1939. Since its beginning, Alcoholics Anonymous has rallied millions of sufferers and become the foundation of their recovery from a fatal, progressive disease over which they had been powerless. Also, A.A.'s Twelve Steps have been modified to create other groups such as Narcotics Anonymous, Overeaters Anonymous, Alanon (which provides hope for the families of those addicted) and Adult Children of Alcoholics. The program has been found effective for type A personalities (those who prefer or find themselves in high-stress jobs), as well as those caught in cycles of violent abuse, compulsive gambling, sexual addiction and other compulsive, addictive or destructive behaviors.

Anyone who admits powerlessness over some troubling aspect of life and is willing to work the Twelve Steps will be rewarded by the fulfillment of the promises. The promises guarantee we will become able to love others and ourselves. The promises guarantee a "new freedom and a new happiness," including peace of mind, freedom from fear, freedom from economic anxieties, new energy, excitement and joy in our lives. This is an offer that is hard to refuse, but which has been almost unknown to all except those in self-help recovery groups. My intention in this book is to make the promises available to everyone.

The Twelve Steps weren't born out of one man's experience, although without Bill W.'s experience we would not have them in their present form. Bill had desperately searched for relief from advanced alcoholism, and probably literally stumbled into the

Oxford Group in New York. The Oxford Group was made up of a number of Christians, mainly Episcopalians, since the movement had sprung from the Church of England. They were trying to capture the spirituality of early Christianity, which they believed secular society had lost. It was a spiritual movement, and their principles were partially based on the exercises of St. Ignatius Loyola, know as the Ignatian Way.

The four principles of the Oxford Group were absolute honesty, absolute purity, absolute unselfishness, and absolute love (*Pass It On*, A.A. World Services, Inc. 1984, p.114). Bill W. spent many hours going over these principles with the Rev. Sam Shoemaker, an Episcopal priest. Through Fr. Shoemaker's guidance and the experiences of many in the initial Alcoholics Anonymous program, these seeds germinated and grew into the Twelve Steps. The Oxford Movement died out, but Alcoholics Anonymous programs flourished. They flourished because of Bill W.'s remarkable discovery that God would do for him what he could not do for himself. In the Twelve Step program, we become willing to "let go and let God."

For a long time I heard and believed that "God helps those who help themselves." I don't know who initially said this but it is tragically wrong. God helps those who recognize they, on their own, can do nothing, and that it is in a loving God that we "live and move and have our being." It is the ill, not the well, who need a physician. Only those who recognize their own powerlessness come to believe God can and will restore them, and become willing to turn their lives over to his care.

Bill W. fleshed out the Twelve Steps in the book *Twelve Steps and Twelve Traditions* (A.A. World Services, Inc., 1952-53, p.15-16. Unless otherwise noted all further quotes are from this reference. It is the author's hope that all those interested in the Twelve Steps will also read this work. It can be purchased from the publisher or from any open A.A. meeting in the community.) and expressed the thought, perhaps the hope, that A.A.'s Twelve Steps could be of use to non-alcoholics while dealing with life's difficulties. A.A. has many little sayings which sometimes sound trite, but which in practice are deeply profound and difficult. One saying is that A.A. isn't for everyone who needs it, but it is for anyone who wants it. The discussion of the Twelve Steps in this book isn't for everyone who needs it; indeed, everyone not already on a spiritual path needs it, but pride makes many reject it. It is for anyone who wants the fruits of the promises: peace, freedom, happiness and especially the peace that comes from loving oneself.

Come along and discover how it works!

—D.M.E.

If I don't like myself, everywhere I go,
there's someone I don't like!

Chapter 1

Many of us don't love ourselves because we didn't "please" someone or measure up to someone's expectations; we weren't the person someone else wanted us to be. Trying desperatly to be perfect, we develop feelings of worthlessness. We spend our lives trying to justify ourselves, attempting to capture self-worth through the approval of others, trying to be pretty or handsome enough, nice enough, smart enough, strong enough, talented enough, rich enough.

Step One — *We admitted we were powerless over _____ [alcohol; drugs; whatever fed our need for self-esteem], that our lives had become unmanageable.*

Pride Misunderstood

The admission of powerlessness comes with a cost most people are unwilling to pay until the last hope of slipping through life without doing so is gone. Even in the face of terrible consequences, some would rather die than pay it. The price is our pride, our most precious commodity. We say of someone, believing it to be a compliment, "Well, she's lost everything, but at least she's got her pride." It's said that only little children can enter the kingdom of heaven, yet as children we yearn to grow up so we can do what we want to do. We want to have power over our lives; we deride those who appear weak. Our heroes are people of power who control those around them through physical, economic, political or sexual advantage. We are beset in childhood with images of little trains who think they can, the "power of positive thinking," charming and strong princes who save the day through personal power, good witches who know the secrets necessary to manipulate elements and gain supernatural power over people, places and things. We are even taught in some churches that God is like a genie in a bottle, who, if we rub him the right way and "have faith," will do what we say, give us what we want. We are taught everywhere not to admit defeat; at all costs to continue to batter the wall with our wills. We are taught that pride is our most valuable asset, our last defense against lost self-worth; poor but proud, proud in defeat, and so on. That we must lose our pride to gain self-worth seems strange.

Spiritually, when we are wrong, we are usually 180 degrees wrong! This is so with pride. Pride separates us from our relationship with God. Pride is the chief deadly sin; we turn it into a virtue! Step One is our first attempt to approach reality, to see ourselves "right size." Usually we fluctuate unrealistically between seeing ourselves as all-powerful or helpless, like Alice in Wonderland, drinking the potion which made her way too big or much too small.

Trying to Get It Right

When we suffer emotional, physical or economic distress, we tend to blame people, places and things for our unhappiness. We blame our society, our parents, our spouses, our children, our bosses, our co-workers, our neighbors, our children's friends, the school, the neighborhood, the town, and on and on. At the deepest level, we blame God, although we usually hide this from ourselves. We believe if we just throw more willpower into the situation, are more crafty in our manipulations, get into a different situation through changes in jobs, spouses, schools, towns, religious affiliations, etc., we will become happy; we believe we will be happy once we get the outside world right! We are sure everything will work, will click, if we can just manipulate people, places and things to be what we want them to be, what we *need* them to be. We approach our environment, including people, from the standpoint of needs to be met.

Our most desperate attempts to manipulate come when our self-image (pride) is threatened. We try to maintain our self-image through the approval of others; we *need* their approval and become "people pleasers." We are fearful of making someone mad, hurting someone's feelings, not for their sake, but because of our own need for their approval. We usually dress up our attempts to meet our need for self-esteem in noble garb, masquerading as "helpers" of others, while we gobble them up in an attempt to justify our own existence, robbing them of their own responsibility and self-esteem. Refusing to be fully justified by being children of God, our attempts at self-justification become all consuming, hopeless, and endless.

Often, all our efforts backfire. Our families, friends, co-workers and bosses revolt; after all, they're trying to do the same thing, trying to manipulate the universe to fit *their* needs. Then, we feel sorry for ourselves, saying no one appreciates our efforts, no one loves us. We don't see that our struggles to find self-esteem through others is the *opposite* of love, as giving to get is the opposite of kindness. When our attempts to make others happy end in our own unhappiness, we can be sure our motive was a selfish attempt to meet our own need for self-esteem.

Although we can't have freedom or happiness without self-esteem, without self-love, pride is truly the opposite of self-esteem, the opposite of self-love. Pride always measures us in relation to something or someone else, so there is always the opportunity for doubt—am I really the best, smartest, richest, prettiest, or at least as good as everyone else? Pride is like the wicked witch in Snow White; never at peace as long as there may be someone or something better. Pride never produces self-esteem; it always provides fearful comparisons.

There once was a woman Beth. Beth was the apple of her mother's eye, but she failed her miserably by marrying the wrong man while still in her teens, thereby destroying the chance for the wonderful career her mother had planned for her. Beth's marriage was hard, ending in divorce; she deeply regretted her mistake. She decided her child, Ann, would have the opportunities she lost, fulfilling both her and her mother's dreams. The child was brilliant, with an exceptionally high I.Q., although she had many problems in school. Beth demanded that Ann excel. She sent her to private schools, hired tutors, bribed, placated, and punished. Ann dropped out of school in the 11th grade, at age 18 married a dropout, married several more times, and has worked in service jobs ever since. Beth is bitterly disappointed in Ann and can't understand "why she wants to throw her life away." Beth fought her way up in her own job and supervises several people of whom she is very critical. Beth doesn't have close friends; she tends to expose the faults of those around her. Beth says she is satisfied with her life, but still tries to help Ann "come to her senses."

Step One for Beth will initially be an admission of powerlessness over Ann and the unmanageability of her own relationships, all of which leave her isolated and alone. As she progresses in the program, she will recognize her powerlessness over her own mother. Finally, she will understand that it is her need for self-justification over which she is powerless.

Powerlessness and Necessity

The paradox is that we believe we are powerless over something necessary for our existence. We intuitively know that in order to live we need self-esteem and self-justification, but we misunderstand their true source. Pride in combination with a genuinely perceived need makes the taking of Step One miraculous; it requires grace. The twin delusions of pride and the expectation of finding self-esteem in people, places and things make intervention a requirement for Step One. Usually, some overwhelming pain is required to break through our delusions and give us a glimpse of reality. This is why rescuing (helping) people from pain caused by their behavior is deadly, and only prolongs and strengthens the delusion, bringing more, worse pain.

Unmanageability = Pain

Step One has two parts; we acknowledge both powerlessness and unmanageability, although in a sense one is an extension of the other. Beth denied both powerlessness and unmanageability. She denied unmanageability by burying her hurt over her daughter's behavior and not acknowledging her anger. She criticized everyone around her to justify herself, creating chilling isolation, but she refused to acknowledge her terrible loneliness and fear.

When we are powerless over our emotions, we use pride to justify them. We feel we're right to be angry, justified in our loneliness, and have good reason to be depressed. We feel misunderstood, mistreated, and maligned. It wouldn't occur to us to recognize powerlessness over such justifiable feelings, yet they imprison us. There are naturally exclusive emotions. Joy and peace cannot abide with anger and fear. Love cannot live with resentment. I cannot resent this one and love that one; resentment darkly colors all my relationships. Fear and anger permeate every situation, and self-justification blinds me to my bonds.

We can sometimes admit powerlessness, but deny we're affected by it. For instance, I'm powerless over anger, depression, anxiety, my child, food, my boss, my spouse, my finances; but I say I don't let it bother me and I go on with my life. I say, "So what, nobody's perfect. Things are tough all over. That's just the way I am." I pretend to mange my unmanageability, because I believe I have done everything possible, thrown every ounce of willpower at my problems, and they have just gotten worse. I feel I have to make the best of a hopeless situation by denying that my anger, fear and disappointment hurt anymore.

Reality intervened in Beth's life when her boss told her she was losing her supervisory job because of her critical attitude toward those under her and her unreasonable expectation that everyone in the organization should perform perfectly. Beth tried mightily to blame others, but her pride was cracked. After her demotion she entered a twelve-step program with an Adult Children of Alcoholics group and began her recovery.

Denial of consequences and denial that the consequences hurt are primary symptoms of pride. I may believe that either the consequences won't happen to me or that I won't be bothered too much by them. I knew a man in A.A. who was still a heavy smoker. He had tried without success many times to quit. When I met him he said he was resigned to his fate. "If I get cancer, I just get cancer," he would say, secretly believing somehow he would be spared the consequences. In spite of the fact that he had used a twelve-step program to relieve his alcoholism, he had never used it for his addiction to nicotine. His relationship to this drug was part of his life he had not been willing to turn over to God.

A few years after I met him and had grown very fond of him, he was diagnosed with lung cancer. He was furious, and immediately asked his higher power to help him quit smoking. He never smoked again, received radiation and chemotherapy, lived a year and died. Yet this story has a happy ending. He died with a deep trust and serenity most never achieve, due to his right relation with his Creator; a relationship that transcends death. Denial of consequences is just as deadly as the denial of powerlessness.

Weakness is Strength

We admit that pain cripples us, and acknowledge that powerlessness is, by definition, unmanageability. Then we let go of our attempt to control the uncontrollable. When we acknowledge our own powerlessness and the unmanageability of our lives, we either despair or look outside ourselves to God.

Bill W. says the only quality needed to take this

step is the capacity to be honest, but that some people lack this capacity; they seem to be born this way. Theologians speak of grace, saying the admission of powerlessness and the ability to see life honestly is a gift from God. Why one becomes honest and another dishonest is a mystery. Our common experience is that in admitting powerlessness, in giving up, we begin to win.

Chapter 2

We intuitively know that to love ourselves we must be loved by someone else. Our problem is that we look for love in all the wrong places, in all the wrong faces.

Betty was alcoholic and had lost everything. She lost her parents through death, her grown children had left her, and her husband was leaving her and taking their young child. She had lost her job, her health and her pride. She had lost everything but God's love.

Step Two — *Come to believe that a Power greater than ourselves could restore us to sanity.*

Coming To

First we "come to." We come out of the delusion that people, places and things will make us happy if we can just "get them right." We have acted as though we were the producer, writer, director, and set designers of our lives. Now we realize we didn't even buy a ticket to the play. We see the reality of our powerlessness over people, places and things, and most profoundly, our powerlessness over our own emotions.

Angels hold their breath, waiting to see if there will be joy in heaven. Here we choose joy or despair. We die in our pride or open our minds to the possibility of a "higher power."

A brilliant young medical resident, Jim, finished his residency and went off to Vietnam to pay his dues to Uncle Sam, leaving behind a young wife and two children. While he was gone, his wife fell in love with a psychiatric resident. When he returned home and discovered his wife wanted a divorce, he became depressed. He brooded over the lives he hadn't saved while in service. He doubted his ability as a surgeon and a man. Jim had considered himself a scientist and believed humanity was the pinnacle of evolution. He had thought there was nothing human beings couldn't achieve. He had believed the universe was a natural process in which the fittest survived; thus perfection would be reached. His beliefs were now dashed; he saw himself as a failure. He committed suicide.

Coming to Believe

Coming to believe in a power greater than ourselves is instantaneous for some; a slower process for others. Belief always comes if we choose life and open our minds.

Looking honestly at the unmanageability of our lives, we may cry, "My delusions of control are shattered, I can't deny my pain. I'm undefended in a hopeless situation. You want to talk about God, but perhaps I don't believe in God. Perhaps I don't trust the God I was taught to believe in. Perhaps I feel I'm not worthy of God's help." Those who work a twelve-step program tell us these statements reveal a mind still closed. They tell us Step Two requires an open mind; exchanging doubt and disbelief for openness means, as Bill W. says, giving up our old ideas completely.

Our intellect may have claimed the evil in the world proves there is no God, or if God exists he either left the scene or is crazy, or we said, "God helps those who help themselves," seeing dependence on God as a sign of weakness or laziness. Perhaps we decided due to our weaknesses and failures we didn't deserve God's help. We may have thought we could do what we wanted with our lives, disregarding God's will with impunity, or we would "do right" when it was easy or fit with our plans, then follow our own will when it seemed expedient to do so. Pride of intellect, pride of self-sufficiency, pride of unworthiness, and pride of defiance can all be overcome, and belief can begin through the simple process of opening our minds.

In or out of prayer, we *always* sought our own will or assumed our will was God's will, which amounted to the same thing. We *never* honestly opened our minds to discover God's will. We never said unconditionally, "Thy will be done." Believing we knew what was good for us, our minds were closed. To come to believe, we have to let go of *all* our old ideas completely, even the idea that we know what we need! Our minds have to become like those of little children, a *tabula rasa*, a blank slate. Once we release our old ideas and open our minds, honestly and willingly asking for help, we get it. There is only one God, and that is the God we discover when we do Step Two.

Tracing Grace

How do people come to a helpful belief in a power greater than themselves, to believe in God? How do they develop a real, practical spirituality? This is a great mystery for those who don't yet believe. How, they wonder, can someone believe in what they can't see, hear or touch? They sometimes dismiss believers as either a little crazy or a little dumb! Then, there are those raised in families where religion is important. They may grow up "believing in God" because they're taught to do so. Growing older, experiencing life's trials, tragedies and temptations, their childish faith is challenged, and sometimes damaged. As people mature, their belief in God must mature, or like a child's toy, it tends to break and is discarded altogether.

People can reach a mature, realistic belief in God by consciously examining their lives and their universe with an open mind. Belief ripens over time as we experience the presence of God through grace in our lives. Those who doubt the existence of God frequently offer the presence of evil in the world as the reason. How, they say, could a loving, powerful

God allow it? Evil, they say, proves there is no all-powerful, all-loving Creator of the universe. Those with an immature faith are shaken by the problem of evil. People who deny God's presence or find God untrustworthy simply haven't viewed their lives in light of all the existing possibilities and alternatives. If they were to open their minds to every possibility, they would see evidence of a caring, involved Providence everywhere. When those who are troubled open their minds, they discover a higher power who can restore them to sanity. For instance, how often did the car not wreck, the plane not crash, or the assault on the dark street not take place? How often did the operation not go wrong, the diagnosis show no cancer, the blood test turn out negative? How often did the dreaded phone call not come in the night, telling us the one we love was ill or hurt or dead. How often did the tornado not strike, or the undertow not drag us out to sea, or the hurricane skip the coast? How often did the iron we left on not start a fire? And how many times did the spouse, parent, sweetheart, neighbor not find out about the dreadful, shameful thing we did or said? Grace is the active presence of God; the presence of a providential power working in our lives for good. Examining the presence of grace in the following five areas can bring us to a more mature, realistic spirituality.

What wonderful thing happened out of many other, perhaps not so wonderful possibilities? Each day has 86,400 seconds. Almost every day of our lives the majority of these seconds are filled with good things—if we have the will to perceive them.

What dreadful thing could have happened, perhaps should have happened, perhaps you even *invited* to happen, but didn't?

What happened which you at first thought was bad, but which wound up having a wonderful result?

What happened that you thought would be the death of you, but you're alive and reasonably O.K.? What would life be like without the real possibility of evil? What good is evil?

What good things have happened to you beginning with your conception? Your mother was born with about one-half million undeveloped eggs in her ovaries, which ripened one-by-one and were randomly released each month after she reached child bearing age. Each male ejaculation contains about 500 million sperm, all of which compete to fertilize the ripened egg. So, excluding all the other instances of sexual intercourse your parents may have shared, at the point of your conception the odds of you rather than someone entirely different being born are about one out of 250,000,000,000,000. And your conception went relatively well. You don't have genetic defects so serious that you can't understand this information. In fact, I suspect that most of you are physically and mentally within normal limits, and even reasonably good-looking—people don't scream and run when they see you. Although your mom may have had the choice, she didn't choose abortion. While you were in her womb, your mother didn't abuse substances causing you to be mentally retarded. While in the womb most of you didn't suffer from illnesses that left you mentally or physically disabled. So after exploring the conceptual and prenatal possibilities, you realize you came out pretty well. You're an amazing, unique individual. You have one or more talents, something only you can do in just that way. You have a wonderful ability to enjoy and contribute to life if you chose to. Grace was present all along.

Now imagine yourself as an infant. You are totally and completely helpless. The only power you have is that of your voice, crying for what you need. Someone took care of you. Although you had nothing to offer in return, you were fed, watered, cleaned, clothed and sheltered. And, since researchers have found that infants won't thrive and will even die without it, you apparently had at least some measure of love. Who did these things? Why did they do them?

As you trace grace in your life, you see it preceding and following you each year as you grew through each stage of development. Grace was there, assuring your safety and providing you with opportunities. Grace sustained you when you were afraid and disappointed, loved you in the smiles, laughter and warm, strong arms of those who cared for you, no matter how imperfect they might have been. Grace provided you with education and experiences, teachers and friends.

Think of the bad things that happened, but which wound up being beneficial. Did you lose the man/

woman you wanted only to find yourself delivered from a terrible fate? Did the job, house, car you desperately wanted not materialize, and you ended up with something more suitable? Did the friend abandon you, allowing you to discover another friendship more real and satisfying? Did you learn something in an illness that made the rest of your life richer and happier than it could have been without the experience? Did someone dear to you die, yet after grieving you found new possibilities of self-discovery and potential? From childhood on, consider the things you dreaded would happen and did, yet which turned out to be to your good.

Now, what about the terrible things you thought would literally kill you should they happen? Things like the death of a spouse or child or parent. Perhaps it was a divorce, or the loss of your home or income. Maybe you were mugged or raped or physically or sexually abused. Before these things happened, you thought that if they happened you would die. Yet, they happened, and you're relatively O.K. You still have fair physical health, and mentally you're able to comprehend and reason. You still have the capacity to love. No matter how terrible the events of the past were, you have interesting and exciting possibilities before you. Unfortunately, some who experience the horrors of loss or abuse use this as positive proof there is no loving, powerful God; they're unwilling to truly trace the grace Providence provides for them. Consider the awful things which happened which you thought would be the death of you, yet you're alive, with the possibility of doors opening to new relationships and with the potential for experiencing and enjoying life.

Why should evil things happen at all, even if they aren't devastating and even if they may turn out to be for our good? Why would a loving, powerful God allow evil in the first place?

• Choice

Without the possibility of real evil there could be no real free will; no meaningful choice. Without free will, you'd be a puppet, a marionette dancing to the commands of a "good" God who didn't allow wrong choices. With free will, you can chose to be a saint or a serial killer, a teacher or a child molester, a Martin Luther King, Jr. or a Hitler; the choice is yours. The most difficult, the most loving gift our Creator gives is freedom.

• Character

Evil reveals character. We learn who we are when we experience evil. Untested, we have no way of really knowing ourselves, knowing what we would do in a pinch, how we would handle the crisis, how we would behave under fire. Would we intervene if we saw someone being attacked? Would we defend our friend if someone lied about him? Would we speak up if someone told a racist joke? Experiencing evil gives us the gift of self-knowledge.

• Challenge

Without evil there would be no challenge. Living in a Garden of Eden, everything would come easily; we'd remain like children, playing at our mother's knee. Without challenge, we'd never grow and develop and learn, we'd never stretch our physical, intellectual and spiritual boundaries.

• Courage

Without evil, there could be no courage. There would be no opportunity to make choices and experience consequences, to fight against the odds, to stand when we have withstood everything, and no opportunity to show great love by giving up our lives for our family, our friends, our country, our beliefs.

• Compassion

Without evil, there would be no compassion, no chance to tenderly suffer with and care for another person, no opportunity, no reason to move outside ourselves, beyond our own selfish concerns, to love, to touch, to share our bounty with another.

So, in a world without evil there would be no choice, no revealed character, no challenge, no courage, and no compassion. The possibility of evil is one of the loving, powerful Creator's greatest gifts. Consider ways your life is blessed because of the real possibility of evil.

Many of us thought we never had enough of anything until we traced grace in our lives and discovered we always had everything we needed. We always had food, shelter and clothing, so that we didn't starve or die from exposure. There was always someone willing to love us if we chose to accept it. In tracing grace, we realize we felt unloved because those willing to love us didn't love perfectly, or they weren't the perfect people whose love we felt we needed and deserved. And we often thought we didn't love anyone because *we* didn't love perfectly. Now, we see that grace fills in the gaps; because of grace, we don't need perfect love from a perfect person, and we don't have to love perfectly in order to love.

No matter what the circumstances, through grace we've always had everything we needed. And grace is the presence of God. With God as our shepherd, we always have and always will have everything we need. Our cup runs over!

Sometimes God is revealed through a mystical epiphany, a life-changing point in time when we have a direct experience of God. This occurs in the lives of ordinary people more often than is commonly realized. Even when a direct experience of God occurs, it's the process of tracing grace that grows the experience into a mature, fruit-yielding plant. Through tracing grace we come to believe in the God who can and will restore us to sanity. And through this assurance, we become ready for Step Three, ready and willing to turn our lives over to this loving power greater than ourselves.

Betty opened her mind. She dropped to her knees in her kitchen one day and unconditionally asked for

God's help. There was no flash of light that day; she was one who came to believe more slowly. She had opened her mind enough for God to throw her a life raft. She entered treatment in a state hospital, something her closed mind would never have considered. Then when she vacillated, wanting to come home before she completed treatment, grace gave her husband strength to ignore her pitiful pleas to come and get her. Grace provided that the A.A. group from her own neighborhood was volunteering at the hospital while she was there, and for the first time she saw sober alcoholics who were peaceful, joyful, grateful and giving. She saw the miracle and she came to believe.

The people Betty saw in A.A. were channels for God's love and peace. Betty saw God in them, a loving God who can and does care for his children. She saw the God who wants to take his children under his wings like a mother hen. She saw that a direct relationship with the living God transcends questions and pain. Like Job, she had heard *about* God but she had never *known* God. Like Job, her pride had made God small and manageable. Now her pride was broken, she related rightly to God as Creator, Sustainer and Redeemer. She was both creature and child. Not all at once, with side trips and pitfalls, and with God's help, Betty is progressing, growing more free, more happy.

God promises that if we knock, he opens; if we ask, we receive. It is not people, places and things God wants to give us; God wants to give us himself, to give us the relationship he made us for. Nothing else brings peace, nothing else will restore us to sanity, because nothing else is absolutely loving, unchangeable and eternal. Everything is nothing compared to this. Only the love of God makes us truly free to love ourselves.

Betty discovered that opening her mind meant, as Bill W. said, "giving up our old ideas completely." She gave up thinking she knew what was good for her and how to get it. Opening her mind meant being born anew as a beloved child of God.

Chapter Three

When we love ourselves because we believe the all-knowing, all-powerful, changeless, eternal Father loves us specially, individually and unconditionally, we quit being our own enemy and turn our lives over to our Creator's care.

John, a military officer, had been in A.A. for a year, but could not stay dry more than a few weeks at a time. He suffered from deep depression, with suicidal thoughts and mental confusion, and couldn't understand what was wrong. He saw A.A. working for others. He thought he had taken the first three steps. He decided he was beyond even God's ability to help.

Step Three — *Made a decision to turn our will and our lives over to the care of God as we understood him.*

Having reached the turning point of Step Two, there are three ways to approach the third step.

We Can't Reject Love

First, we may decide the price is too high. We may understand the requirements of this step and refuse to take it. We become angry with a God who self-ishly requires us to give up all aspects of our lives to his care. We may resent a Creator who creates totally dependent creatures. We want to count for something! We want to make some decisions, take action on our own without having our personalities disappear into the will of God. We feel like we'll become the smile on the Cheshire cat, the hole in the donut. Why, we ask, would God create us with intellects and personal strengths if he didn't expect us to use them!

Pete was such a person. He was involved in sexual practices even the most liberal of us might call unhealthy, and would certainly call unloving, and his sponsor advised him to give them up. Pete wasn't willing. He held tightly to the belief that whatever consenting adults did sexually was all right, and it wasn't God's or anyone else's business. Of course, this meant Pete had slipped all the way back to Step One, since he was addicted to these practices in addition to alcohol and drugs. Sadly, he will have to suffer again. The cocoon of pride God ripped open through adversity re-closed before Pete made the decision to step outside.

Accepting a Little Love

Second, we may delude ourselves, thinking we can turn just some part of our lives over to the care of God, the part that troubles us, and keep mastery over the rest. We ask God to help us with "this," while we control everything else. We don't realize we are patronizing God, nor do we see how comical we look. Here we have the Creator of the universe, with infinite wisdom and omnipotence, the Author of Love, personally offering to care for us, and we say, "you can have this part, but I'd rather handle the rest myself."

Pride calls this reasonable. From God's point of view, it is foolishness. Christ himself said the One who sent him was greater than he. Christ claimed all he did was the will of the Father. He said he and the Father were One, because he always submitted to God's will. He made no claims for himself. He said he came to serve, not to be served. To pride, this seems crazy. The Pharisees said Jesus had a "demon," meaning he was insane. Right reason and honesty tell us God's will is always better for us than our own; God loves us perfectly, seeing what we can't with our limited vision, knowing what we can't with our limited understanding. And, since God's will is always and only love for us and all creation, God works everything out for our good.

John had unknowingly diverged from his progression through the steps by making the second choice. His military training as an officer had ingrained in him the need to be competent in a crisis, to make independent decisions. He was successful in his military career until alcoholism began to interfere. He had received medals, commendations and promotions of which he was proud. He saw no reason to turn anything over to God except the drinking problem, certain he could handle everything else.

Surely the step didn't mean to turn *everything* over to God.

When John tried life without alcohol, feelings and realities surfaced. He found he was estranged from his wife and hadn't known it. He was angry and resentful toward his superiors, who seemingly had forgotten all his successes and were now persecuting him for his one weakness. He felt the military was hypocritical and ungrateful, trying to throw him away without his pension after he had sacrificed so much for his country. He realized he had no relationship with, didn't even know, his children, who were now grown and had left home.

In treatment after a suicide threat, John discovered he had not really been willing to take Step Three. He made a decision to turn his will and his life, including his mental and emotional life, over to God.

Step Three, like all the other steps, must be repeated again and again, because we humans tend to change our mind. We make the decision and turn over our will and life, our thoughts and emotions, to God's will one day, then the next day, or week, or month we may take them all back again. But practice leads to progress; with each repetition we may consciously turn over more and more of our will to God. There is a big difference between unconsciously reserving some of our own will, and consciously withholding some part of our lives. In the first case, we may continue along the steps; in the second case, we fall back to Step One.

Accepting Love

In our first story, Beth made the third choice, turning her will and life over to God. In early recovery, she saw her attempts to control her daughter as her primary problem. Sometime later she saw her unsuccessful attempts to please her mother as something to turn over, something of which she was not initially conscious. Finally, working Step One again, she found the root of her powerlessness was her need to justify herself, and fully accepted God's love as justification. Each new Step One insight made each new third step more complete, bringing greater peace, freedom and happiness. Beth reconciled with herself, and loving herself, ceased being her own enemy.

This is "a program of progress, not perfection." We never become perfect, but we continue to make spiritual progress as long as we faithfully and *honestly* follow the steps. Pretending doesn't count, it only binds us more tightly in our delusions. Bill W. says this program requires "rigorous honesty." Such honesty is foreign to most of us. Honesty is the enemy of pride. Christ says he is Truth, and Satan is the father of lies. Christ *is* Truth; we *approach* truth. Pride has many tentacles, and like trick candles on a birthday cake, as soon as we think they're all out, one flares up again.

Step Three involves giving up our lives and wills to the care of God, which includes our emotions. Keeping the open mind we attained in Step Two, we become willing to let God tell us how we should feel.

Before, we felt justified in our angry resentments, believing we needed anger and resentment to protect us in a hostile world. When we turn our lives over to God's care, we no longer need these defenses. With no further need to protect ourselves, we can put away our boxing gloves. The loss of our defensive posture is a clear sign that we have *really* begun Step Three. There are layers of defenses, just as there are layers of disguised pride. Dropping our defenses is like peeling a many-layered onion. We must be thorough if we are to receive the promises of the program—"a new freedom and a new happiness" through which we lose our fear of people and economic insecurity. I have known many people in twelve step programs who felt that since they could never reach perfection, they could be less than rigorous in their approach. They never achieved the promises and left, saying the program doesn't work.

Love is Personal

We turn our will over to the *God of our understanding*. Trust is the goal of Step Two, when we come to believe God can and will restore us to sanity. In Step Two, we began our own personal relationship with our higher power. God speaks to each of us individually; his relationship with each of us is unique. It's as if each of us were God's only child. Our relationship with God is more private than that of a husband and wife. There is always a mystery in the marital relationship into which not even children or parents can enter. No outsider can "get inside" the relationship between spouses, and this is even truer in our relationship with God. We can never trust someone else's understanding of God to the extent that we must to take Step Three. I have mentioned Christ and I am a Christian, but when I began my twelve step program I had no theological notions, only the hope that there was a God who could and would help me. God did.

God is alive, able and willing to relate to his children. My A.A. experience tells me God doesn't especially care what you call him. As a matter of fact, I could even call him her since God transcends gender. God's main concern is that we give up the delusions, the illusions, the idols we hoped would save us—including ourselves—and enter into reality; reality is the Kingdom of Heaven. God is God, and doesn't have to worry about names. "I Am" will do. When all our idols of people, places and things—children, spouses, parents, jobs, titles, prizes, houses, being nice, our own self-esteem—are gone, God still *is*. We do need a way, some touchstone, to be sure we stay honest and oriented, because of our tendency to have flare-ups of pride and defensiveness as the layers peel off. Some of these anchors will be mentioned in Step Eleven. God is the only God there is, and he will lead us into relationship with him if we become willing. This is the greatest freedom and happiness; it is for this that we were created!

Life Spilling Over

God gave us intellect, reason and will so that *we* can make the decision. We do not disappear when we turn our wills and lives over to God's care; rather, giving up delusion for reality, leaving off people-pleasing, losing our fear of economic insecurity and feelings of hopelessness and worthlessness, we become truly exceptional individuals through our relationship with him. God loves diversity. He never creates the same thing twice. Recently I observed the hatching of a Mallard duckling. I watched the baby emerge from the egg, and as it dried, I noticed that each little down feather was different from the other, and realized this little duck was different from all other ducks hatched since the beginning of time. Also, there has never been anyone like me before, and never will be again. My relationship with God is personal. My relationship affirms my personality rather than diminishes it. No longer is my cup half empty or half full—now it runs over. In my new freedom that comes from authentic self-love, I'm free to be uniquely me.

Step Three is necessary for continued spiritual progress. It does no good to try to skip ahead to other steps; they can't be done successfully without a genuine attempt at Step Three.

"Nothing's changed, but everything's different." This expression defines the experience of making the decision of Step Three. We discover boredom was a symptom of depression; when we're depressed, nothing is exciting, nothing is interesting, nothing is beautiful (depressed people can't stop and smell the roses; they can't see the roses). We struggled but failed to find meaning in our lives. Now the world is beautiful, full of interesting, exciting people, places, and things. Even sitting on the porch, petting the dog, talking with our spouse is filled with meaning.

The decision is a spiritual action wherein having come to believe in a living, loving God with whom we can be in relationship, and whose power is greater than ours, we finally give up our own unhappy struggle to run the show for ourselves and others, and turn over our whole selves—physical, intellectual, emotional, and spiritual—to the God of our understanding. It is only to the "God of our understanding" that we can be willing to turn. We trust and believe the God we understand, for this is the One with whom we have found a unique, personal relationship. Now we are truly free to be ourselves.

Here I need to remind those who have decided to work this program that few of us immediately make the decision of Step Three. In my own case, I attended A.A. meetings and enjoyed the fellowship, but saw no need to personally work the steps or get a sponsor (someone familiar with the program who acts as a spiritual guide). I thought the steps and sponsors were fine for those who needed them; I was bright enough and spiritual enough not to. As a result, for one and one-half years I never attained emotional sobriety or lasting abstinence. Finally, powerless and unmanageability broke my pride. I opened my mind, came to believe, and made the decision. In the working of all these steps the motto is, "Easy does it, but darn it, do it." There is no hurry, but the longer it takes, the longer we suffer, hating ourselves, justifying ourselves, hiding from God like Adam and Eve, ashamed and afraid.

Does the decision of Step Three mean nothing "bad" will ever happen to us again? Of course not. Things got about as "bad" as bad can get for Christ. He was unjustly derided, tortured, and cruelly executed—after being deserted by those he loved most. Paul says in Romans 8:26-39 that all things work together for good for those who love God. He goes on to say we will experience trials, persecutions, tribulations, and worse, but nothing, absolutely nothing can come between us and God's love. Nothing in life or death, on heaven or earth, none of the forces of the universe, nothing in all creation can separate us from the love of God.

In this promise lies the peace that passes understanding by the rest of the world, the peace the world counts as foolishness. When we come to believe, we believe that God, because he loves us, will always work out everything for our good from his eternal point of view. The thing I may dread the most and see as the worst that could happen, God, from the point of view of my eternal happiness, may see as my good. Because I believe God works all things together for my good, I turn over my will and life to his care.

Chapter Four

Good always overcomes evil by continuing to love. The higher power is unchanging. God, because of his nature, always loves us. If our character defects could cause God to stop loving us, then his nature would change and evil could overcome good. Love covers the multitude of sins. God has already known us completely, judged us and declared us lovable. Our judgment of ourselves is what kept us alienated, alone and afraid. To continue our movement toward self-love we must face our character defects.

Vernelle was a slight man who loved motorcycles. He didn't ride with others; he was a solitary rider. Vernelle hadn't stayed long in school. His father had been an abusive alcoholic and his mother a hard working, uneducated woman who tried to "hold the family together." Even as a child, Vernelle was small, and he didn't have a home conducive to study. At school, he was always the object of derision and was always in trouble, so when he began to absent himself early in his school career, it wasn't surprising. Vernelle's behavior gave his father further occasion to be abusive and drink, and "broke his mother's heart," but no one else cared. Rather, the school was relieved to see him go.

In spite of all this, Vernelle had hoped to be a good

man, a good husband and father. He married young and had several children. But he was genetically doomed from both his father and his overweight mother's side, both coming from families riddled with chemical dependency, and he began to drink at an early age. He soon found alcohol and employment didn't mix, and was frequently fired. He finally gave up on work since he was powerless over alcohol, lived on the streets estranged from his family, and was often arrested. His wife had him committed to the state hospital many times to "dry out." His children feared and hated him.

Step Four — *Made a searching and fearless moral inventory of ourselves.*

There are five key words in this step, each of which is vitally important if we are to receive the promises of a new freedom and a new happiness. They are *fearless, searching, moral, inventory* and *ourselves*.

Fearless

Challenged to look at ourselves and our own behavior, our first impulse is to flee. How many of us approach any review of our work by others with total confidence? Even if we know we've done an outstanding job, there's a lurking fear that we may hear criticism. We all long to be perfect, or to justify our imperfections by blaming them on other people places or things, or to show that other people are even less perfect than we are. As a matter of fact, most of our character defects, those aspects of ourselves we search out in our moral inventory, are the result of this need to be perfect or justified through the imperfections of others. *Self-justification is our primary enemy.*

It came as a surprise to me several years ago to learn that even the most base criminals either believed themselves innocent or justified in their behavior. Child molesters genuinely believed the children enjoyed and needed the experience of love they provided; they felt misunderstood and maligned by society. Those who conned old people out of their savings justified this by believing the old people deserved it because, like everyone else, they were trying to cheat by making a "fast buck" with their investment or get something expensive for very little. Being the wife of a prison chaplain opened my eyes to the ease with which we can justify the most abhorrent behavior. If we can rationalize such huge character defects, think how easily we justify what we consider small ones.

Our greatest fear—the anathema of the human race—is discovering and accepting our limitations—and we may go to any length to avoid this. The terrible knowledge discovered by Adam and Eve in the garden was the knowledge that they were not God. They had been like infants in the crib; everything was part of them and they were part of everything. The baby thinks the mother is part of itself. It has no ego boundaries, it cries and thinks this action magically makes mother come. The discovery that we are finite, limited, relatively powerless, imperfect individuals, as opposed to the omniscient, omnipresent, omnipotent God is unacceptable. This is why God in his love and mercy wanted us not to discover this. We're unwilling to live with the reality that we are creatures and not the creator. Either we deny our faults, or we blame God for them, as Adam did, saying the woman *God* gave him caused the problem. Adam blamed the woman, but ultimately blamed God for making and giving him such a flawed companion. This is a subtle trick by which we become superior to God, *we* become God's judge! God made the universe wrong. We uncover God's character defects, not our own.

In order, then, to take a fearless moral inventory we must first take Steps One, Two, and Three. Fearlessness can only come when we believe God loves us personally, individually, and unconditionally in spite of our limitations and our history of unloving acts and attitudes towards other human beings as well as creation in general. Confidence that God's love can't be altered by our actions releases us from fear.

Searching

Our inventory must also be searching if we want to find the peace of the promises. We must look in every corner, behind every door, under every rug, in every closet. In each past relationship, over the entire course of our lives we must identify where we were angry or resentful and determine what character defect caused our discomfort. We must see where we were wrong, and if it still seems that our discomfort was caused by other people, we must see why we couldn't accept things as they were.

We begin to understand that it's not the actions of others that trouble us, it's our own fear and insecurity, our own desire to control the uncontrollable. We see that anger is always a disguise for fear; we see a situation that frightens us, and the decision is limited to standing, fighting, or fleeing. If we flee, we call it fear; if we fight, we call it anger. Actually, whether we fight or flee, we prefer to call it anger; it makes us seem stronger. No matter what we call it, fear is what we get when we don't trust God. What we called "righteous" anger is our conscious or unconscious attempt to blame God for allowing evil, our way of rising above God, trusting in our own limited vision rather than his infinite goodness. Our tendency is always to disguise our character defects, dressing them up in more attractive garb, making our search difficult. We disguised pride, dressing it up to look like righteousness.

As we make our searching inventory, we discover that our character defects were the very defenses we thought were necessary to survival in a hostile world. Every time we lied, cheated, stole, assassinated the character of others through gossip, judged others, misbehaved sexually or with substances, it was an attempt to satisfy a need we feared would not be met in more acceptable ways. We always acted in order to defend ourselves from loss or pain, or to get what we thought we needed, and couldn't get in more acceptable ways. The feared loss could be material, economic, or loss of ego through self-judgment or judgment by others. The need can be physical as in addiction, chemical and/or behavioral, but it can also be the need for financial security, self-esteem, or the esteem of others. The search, in a sense, is endless and requires a lifetime. As we grow spiritually, we become more adept at seeing through the disguises we craft for our character defects, so what seems all right today, we may recognize as a serious fault in a few years. Each time we take Step Four, the search must be as complete as possible. If we knowingly repress or skip over anything, our peace won't be complete.

Moral

Our inventory must be moral. This means that we did something which harmed ourselves or others, and that the act was purposeful, volitional. We acted selfishly to meet our needs at some cost to others. Interestingly, some of our acts which appear selfless may be selfishness in disguise. When we try to get or keep love or affirmation by absorbing pain others should feel as a consequence of their behavior, we're really acting selfishly. God sets consequences in place for unloving behavior towards ourselves or others. We act immorally when we interfere with someone's suffering such consequences because we "can't stand to see someone in pain." Once again, this means we're judging God and not trusting him.

We do not need to be concerned with acts which harmed ourselves or others through ignorance or our natural limitations, and not out of fear that our needs won't be met. Some of us tend to be melancholy and see everything we do as wrong. This is pride in reverse, but still pride. Often at meetings I hear people say, "I'm the world's worst _____," and realize they haven't come right size yet. As far as pride is concerned, there is no difference between "I'm the world's worst," and "I'm the world's best." For those who tend to disguise pride as humility (being right size), it may be helpful to inventory our good qualities as well as our moral failures. The seven deadly sins are pride, anger, lust, sloth, envy, greed, and covetousness; but fear is the foundation, the cornerstone, the driving force behind them all.

Inventory

The inventory should be written. I resisted this, so did Vernelle. When an inventory is taken everything is included, nothing is left out. Writing our inventory helps us be thorough; with a written inventory we don't go around in endless circles, never sure we've included everything. In this case we are taking stock of ourselves and must omit nothing. Writing the inventory makes it manageable. Finally we can say, "That's all." The written word traps reality and locks it in. Now we no longer tremble over what may be in the closed closet. Now we have opened the door and turned on the light. There may be a mess there, but it's a manageable mess, and the nameless terror is gone. Once we complete Steps Four and Five, the need for self-justification and justification by others will be gone. We lose our fear of people, and lose the need to please them through dishonesty.

Ourselves

Until now we have always made "searching moral inventories" of others, including God, but when the spotlight turned on us we disguised, rationalized, minimized, and blamed people, places and things for our shortcomings. Working Step Four, for the first time we eliminate the word "blame" from our spiritual vocabulary and accept responsibility. We saw ourselves as victims of circumstances, well-intentioned people caught up in events out of our control, dropped into a hostile world where we had to protect ourselves and struggle to survive. If we ever did the wrong thing, it was for the right reason. The reasons were that the person—the woman, man, child, parent, boss, co-worker, friend, etc.—God gave me was bad; therefore, I was bad. From Adam on, taking a moral inventory of ourselves without blaming God and others was impossible. Now God's grace makes us able to do it.

Vernelle had been dry in A.A. for eleven years. He went to at least one meeting every day. He bragged that since he hadn't gone to school much he couldn't count very well, so when he was told to make 90 meetings in 90 days, he had to just keep on going. Vernelle was deeply involved in the fellowship; he held office in the kind of haphazard way A.A. provides for office holding. He did twelve step work and held the battered heads of many an alcoholic. He spoke at meetings and sponsored people. But Vernelle had never really taken the Fourth Step. He said it was unnecessary to write down all that garbage; you just needed to know you had been generally asinine. So many of the "bad" things he had done were public record, he minimized the need to look further. He used his illiteracy as a rationalization, but the reality was that he still feared looking into his heart.

Throughout all the years of crazy drunkenness, Vernelles's wife had not divorced him. Now she was divorcing him. He complained bitterly of her faults and pretended to be happy about the divorce, giving him an opportunity to become a "ladies' man." In reality, Vernelle grieved for his wife and in spite of all his talk, he never pursued any ladies. Desperate, he finally became willing to listen to his own sponsor who had told him for years to do a real fourth step. (Good A.A. sponsors are very patient people due to their valuable self-knowledge.) With the help of his sponsor, Vernelle began to see that his life had been characterized by selfishness, both before and since being in A.A. He had always put his own interests first, and never even wondered what his wife and children might want or need. The times when he had seemed most concerned as a husband and father were due to his selfish desire to *appear* to be a good husband and father, thereby justifying himself in some small way. His overtures and proclamations of love had been an attempt to get his wife and children to meet his own need for self-esteem. Never, as Bill W. tells us in *Twelve Steps and Twelve Traditions*, had he been willing to be one in a family of others. His family had been objects to be manipulated to meet his needs. Vernelle found this insight humiliating (humility-producing). Now he could proceed along the rest of the steps, accepting forgiveness and making amends.

It was very hard for Vernelle to give up his habit of blaming others for his woes. He had been taught to do so by his parents (his mom had blamed his dad and his dad, his mom), by his teachers, by his counselors, ministers and psychiatrists. Everyone seemed to have colluded to keep Vernelle from accepting responsibility for his defects of character. That he became willing was due to the fact that God lovingly, mercifully, set up painful consequences, and because he had taken the prior steps.

A sadder story is that of Margaret. She, too, was in A.A. for many years, but never attained emotional sobriety. Margaret was a southern aristocrat with a physician husband. She was the only child of older parents, the delight of their lives. She could do no wrong. Her father was alcoholic, and in time she, too, sank deeply into alcoholism. Over the years her husband and children became alienated. Her husband was finally divorcing her. Whenever her sponsor mentioned the need for a moral inventory, she responded that it was others who were at fault, and if her sponsor really understood her and cared about her, she would give her advice on how to change her husband and children to make her life less painful.

Margaret drifted away from A.A., having never come to believe in a God she could trust with her will and life. She never opened her mind.

As we take a searching and fearless moral inventory of ourselves, we're surprised to discover that the sources of our emotional insecurities—worry, anger, self-pity and depression—are our own character defects rather than the fault of other people, places and things. We find our own defenses have ambushed us spiritually and emotionally. The rewards for a thorough Step Four are new understanding, confidence, and renewed relationships. As we stop blaming others and take responsibility for our own defensiveness, our relationships improve. Amazingly, *as we improve spiritually, those around us seem to get better as well.*

Chapter Five

Sacraments are outward and visible signs of inward and spiritual grace. Everything we do is an outward and visible sign of the presence or absence of God's grace working within us. Because we are physical people in a material world, the acts we do match and reveal our spiritual condition. Our actions give substance to what—without the actions—might just be our imagination. A.A. speaks of talking the talk without walking the walk. The Bible speaks of faith without works being absent or dead. In the fifth step we walk the walk. The fifth step provides proof to ourselves that we love ourselves.

Jimmy, a homosexual, was a nurse in military service who had a faithful and loving relationship with his present partner, but who had been promiscuous in the past. Jimmy realized he was homosexual in early adolescence, but painfully hid it from everyone. It was his secret; not even his closest friend knew. He guarded his secret for many years, until he was sent overseas. There, he felt anonymous. He started drinking, going from bar to bar in the evening. He found that alcohol released his inhibitions, and he began to pick up males for sex. In his heart, though, he was ashamed of this behavior, and he worried that the military authorities would find out and he would lose his career. He decided to quit drinking and with great effort of will did so. One day, after an almost sleepless night, feeling terribly angry and depressed, he stole a patient's Darvon to ease the pain and get some sleep. Quickly, Jimmy became addicted to opiates, and returned to bars and anonymous boys. When he came home to the states, Jimmy feared his promiscuous behavior would surely cost him his job and possibly get him hurt. Also, the behavior still racked him with guilt. He found a partner he cared for and settled down into a quiet life. Jimmy had successfully hidden his most shameful episodes. However, he came up positive on a drug screen and was placed in the Army's alcohol and drug recovery program.

Step Five — *Admitted to God, to ourselves and to another human being the exact nature of our wrongs.*

Promises Coming True

We are naturally fearful of this step and may want to rebel. It's fine to turn our lives and wills over to God and to take inventory, but telling another human being our worst faults seems dangerous and unnecessary. Here, the minds of many of us snap shut again and we refuse to allow the steps to be our teacher. If we close up permanently we remain isolated from our fellow human beings and never experience the freedom and happiness the steps promise. We remain afraid of people and continue to manipulate them for our self-justification. Many who come to twelve step programs and don't clearly see the value of Step Five do it because they trust the experience of others. They reap the step's benefits.

"We are as sick as our secrets," is a term often used in addiction treatment settings, but it applies to us all. People have known from antiquity that "confession is good for the soul." For two thousand years, telling character defects to another person has been a religious act. With the advent of modern psychotherapy, other secular professionals discovered the efficacy of telling another human being the exact nature of one's wrongs. As long as we have something to hide, something so shameful we never want another person to know about it, we can't be fully open. As long as we have a guilty secret we hoped to take to our grave, we fear someone will discover it. As long as we fear others, we can't achieve the psychological and emotional balance the steps promise. Guilt and fear are viruses that infect *all* of our relationships, making us unable to reach out freely in love to other persons.

Honestly working Step Five brings the new freedom and new happiness of the promises. Almost magically we no longer see people as objects to fear or manipulate, but as brothers and sisters to love. We quit taking inventory of others' faults; instead, we see them as imperfect persons beset by errant emotions, no different from ourselves. We no longer take hurts "personally," understanding that others are only trying—driven by fear—to meet their own needs. We realize evil is never directed personally towards the victim—its origin is the deep need of the evildoer, and anyone at all who might be able to satisfy that need will do. Need breaks people into parts, seeing only the piece which may satisfy the need. Need says, "He's handsome; if he likes me, it will boost my self-esteem." Need says, "She's rich, if she marries me my fear of economic insecurity will leave." Counter-intuitively, some people, especially those who suffer from depression, need to affirm the negative; they like for the outside to match the inside, they look for evil, lies and ugliness rather than goodness, truth and beauty. In their case, need might say, "She's selfish. If I get into relationship with her, she'll meet my need to be treated badly," or "He's dumb and ugly. If I get in a relationship with him, it will meet my need to confirm my worthlessness." Only love is personal; love never acts out of need.

Victims of abusers are easily exchangeable, anyone willing to stay and absorb the abuse will do. Rapists don't care whom they rape; there is nothing personal in their attack. We see that the angry outbursts of others are not our fault, just as our own angry outbursts were not the fault of others—we know anger is always the expression of personal fear. Having experienced forgiveness from God and another human being, having been justified by God's love for us with no further need for self-justification, we recognize that others manipulated us in a desperate attempt to justify themselves. We now feel kindred with, and sympathy for, those who haven't yet begun their spiritual walk. We are prepared for further development.

There are at least four excellent rationales working the fifth step. The first is that it continues the work begun in Step Four; it collapses our character defects down closer to "right size." Even when written down, our defects may still look formidable until we share them with another person. It's like making what you think is a terrible mistake, telling someone about it, and hearing him say, "Oh, is that all?" We take ourselves far too seriously, on both the debit and credit side. Remember from Step Three how St. Paul tells us that *nothing* can separate us from the love of God; nothing in all creation, nothing in heaven, nothing on earth or under the earth, not death itself can separate us from God's love! God's love overcomes the worst we have done or can ever do. Talking over our character defects with another person helps us stop making them too large or too small.

Reconciliation with Others

The second benefit of the fifth step is that telling another person the exact nature of our wrongs gives that person a chance to share a helpful truth with us; he or she had many of the same defects. Not one of us has invented an original sin. As human beings we share the same fear of unmet needs, although we express our fear in a variety of ways. We see the human heart is, indeed, wicked once the disguises are removed. We understand there is no qualitative difference between us and "hardened criminals." We know that pride is the chief sin and we've all had plenty of it! So when we tell our deep, dark secrets to another, we find our sins are fairly common, not unique at all. We lose our fear of people and join humanity in fellowship and love.

Reconciliation with Ourselves

Third, by taking Step Five we unite with ourselves. There are no longer parts of us we have to deny or disguise or hide. We become integrated. We become whole persons. Until now, we felt incomplete, trying to make ourselves whole through relationships with others or with the outside environment. We had grabbed on to people, places and things, fearfully clinging to them in a desperate, doomed effort to complete our personalities. A joke in A.A. is that practicing alcoholics don't have relationships, they take hostages. A similar joke circulates in Alanon, the program for family and friends of alcoholics. It goes, "To find out if a bird loves you, you have to open the cage. If it flies away and then comes back to you, that's love. Alanons never let the bird go, and if it escapes, they hunt it down and kill it." These may seem like grim jokes to the uninitiated, but people making spiritual progress have learned not to take things seriously (more about this in chapter eleven). Having moved beyond some of our worst defects, we can see them humorously. Prior to taking Step Five we always felt alone, even in a crowd of friends, even with those we loved. We made desperate attempts to enhance our identity through our children, spouses, jobs, churches and organizations because we were split off from part of ourselves, and were incomplete. Now we can relax. *We have become whole people entirely through God's love for us, and are no longer lonely, not even when we're "alone."*

Reconciliation with God

Fourth, and most important, taking Step Five opens us to greater humility, bringing us into a truer relationship with God. We could never "see" God because we never wanted to; we had turned away. We didn't want to see how small, how insignificant, how powerless we were in relationship to the Creator. The benefit of humility is that it allows us to turn around and "see " God, joyfully acknowledging that in ourselves we are nothing. It's in God that we live, move and have our being; yet we are of infinite value because of God's love for us; he calls us his children. Pride tells us we need not, we dare not open our hearts to another human being; humility leads us forward. Pride tells us our egos will be shattered and we will put ourselves in great danger by taking the fifth step. Trust in the God of our understanding gives us courage to proceed.

Jimmy never took the fifth step. His life-long habit of keeping secrets prevailed. He never trusted another person to understand him. Pride insisted his case was too sordid, too shameful to disclose. He remained isolated, full of fear, and eventually returned to drug use. Jimmy was caught taking drugs intended for a patient, declared a failure in his treatment program and discharged from the service.

God doesn't make spiritual progress more difficult for one than for another. We all have guilty secrets. Some may appear more destructive or more disgusting than others, but each of us feels the same amount of guilt. We judge ourselves just as harshly if we have psychologically or emotionally abused or neglected a child as we do if we have physically or sexually abused a child. We can be as ashamed and disturbed over our hatred of our spouses as does someone who murdered a spouse. Our fear of others can feel as shameful as our aggression toward others. This is what Christ means when he says the thought is equal to the deed. It wasn't that Jimmy's "sins" were any worse than anyone else's. His inability to take Step Five came from his inability to withhold judgment of himself and allow God to be the judge. You may have heard the saying that a physician who treats himself has a fool for his doctor. Well, someone who judges her/himself has a fool for a magistrate.

When taking Step Five, we must be careful about our confidant. We want someone who has worked a twelve-step program, or who has by other means achieved spiritual progress through the process of self-evaluation and the sharing of personal defects. We do not want a spiritually immature person who will either feel superior or encourage minimization, rationalization or self-justification. Unfortunately, many clergy, counselors, psychiatrists and friends tend to do either or both.

We also want someone we can trust. Again, spiritual maturity is the only personal quality that assures trustworthiness. Sometimes out of fear and pride we confide in someone because we "feel comfortable" with them, or we "identify with them," thinking we can talk to them more easily because they share our defects. Then we may find our confidant blackmailing us emotionally or sharing our secrets with others. The "fruits" of spiritual maturity are peace, happiness and freedom, with selfless love for our fellow men and women. Those who have made enough spiritual progress to be trusted with our fifth step judge no one; they aren't critical or angry or rigid. When we see these qualities, we can be sure we have the right person.

It's wise to ask God's help in discerning the proper person. We learn about people by watching their actions rather than by listening to their words. Once again, the guideline for action is "easy does it, but darn it, do it!"

Step Five is one of the most difficult steps, so it's also one of the most freeing. Pride shrinks and humility grows with each step along the twelve-step path. Each step brings us into a closer relationship with God. Step Five gives us the ability to accept and to give forgiveness, a sense of kinship with creation, and oneness with self and with God. Step Five restores our ability to love.

Chapter Six

When we didn't love ourselves and were estranged from ourselves, when we were our enemy, we thought we had lots of unmet needs. Now that we are becoming whole, the feeling of neediness is easing. The less we feel we need, the less we need defenses.

A woman named Jane was in a twelve-step program for families. She was emotionally estranged from her husband but was still living with him. Her children were grown and married. Jane had "fallen in love" with a man in the program, and was having an affair with him. She felt hopeless about her relationship with her husband, but feared divorce. The man with whom she was having the affair hadn't said he wanted to marry her, and she was economically dependent. She rationalized staying with her husband by believing he couldn't survive without her. She felt caught up in forces beyond her control. She knew the affair was wrong, but thought she deserved some affection and happiness.

A second story is Jerry's. He had been in a twelve-step program many years and took great pride in helping others—he thought—unselfishly. He took boys who were in trouble and had no place to go into his home. Jerry attended every twelve-step meeting available and encouraged others to do so. Although he praised the program and the steps, I seldom saw him at the special weekly meetings where each step was discussed. I frequently encountered him at discussion meetings, however, and he usually commented on the misbehavior of the young people he had taken in; they had vandalized his property, lied to him, stolen his goods, etc., but stated that this didn't affect him because of the peace provided by the program.

A third story is John's. His father worked his way up in society from humble beginnings, but never felt completely comfortable in the social circles to which his wealth admitted him. John never felt truly good enough either. He went to college, but his grades kept him from getting into graduate school, so he wasn't able to pursue the profession his dad wanted for him. He did, however, discover alcohol and cocaine in college, and the feelings they provided. John went into treatment again and again, but never seemed to be able to get the program right; he hasn't yet recovered.

Step Six — *We are entirely ready to have God remove all these defects of character.*

God does not come into our lives and wrench away our character defects. He allows us to keep those we want or—which is the same thing—feel we need. This is a great surprise to many who expect that once confessed, character defects dissolve like bad dreams.

Back to the Past

Our character defects were our defenses in a hostile world. We never take a perfect Step Three, and so we never become willing to give up all of our character defects, but we can make prodigious progress. While we never reach perfection in trusting God, we can certainly approach it. The closer we come to perfect trust, the less we fear and the less we feel the need of defenses to protect ourselves. The more perfectly we believe, as did the Psalmist, that the Lord is our refuge and our sure defense, the more we find that our own defenses were inadequate and actually increased our anxiety and fear.

Becoming entirely ready to have God remove these defects means just that, we must become *entirely* ready. Being somewhat ready won't suffice. God always waits until we become entirely ready to rely on him before he removes our defenses.

Some of our defects/defenses are so enjoyable we hate to give them up. We were proud of our dripping sarcasm, believing it put us far above the crowd by demonstrating our quick wit and wry sense of humor. We thought it really did no one any permanent damage and those who bore the brunt of it deserved it.

We believed our anger with our family members not only justified, but necessary to keep them from running all over us. Overpowering everyone with rage seemed useful, even enjoyable, and we felt we would be powerless and vulnerable if we had to give it up.

Gossip, the act of murder by character assassination, had seemed a harmless pleasure. What in the world would we talk to people about if we couldn't engage in a little gossip? Gossip was an integral part of social life, and people would think we were strange if we didn't participate.

Being critical of others seemed beneficial as long as it was honest and direct. If it hurt, well, the truth often did hurt. It was our obligation to point out others' shortcomings.

Having resentments toward others seemed to be a real protection. If you forgot what others did to you, you would always be vulnerable to attack. We said, "I may forgive it, but I'll never forget it."

We rationalize our sexual misbehavior, pretending it's really all right since through the faults of others we've been deprived of love. We feel God doesn't really expect us to go through life without getting our emotional/sexual needs met; otherwise why would he have given us needs to begin with?

Being totally honest at work might cause us to lose the promotion we feel we deserve, making us unable to give our family members all the things they deserve. We're sure God doesn't expect our spouses and children to suffer in order for us to walk the "straight and narrow."

All the old fears, like replays of old tapes, creep back to stop us from being willing to have God remove our defects. We are unable to envision ourselves stripped of the defenses we relied on so long. We are limited human beings; we are powerless over our inability to hold on long to an idea or concept. We're especially quick to forget who we are and what we've learned spiritually. Our understanding of deep spiritual concepts can be forgotten in minutes, *in seconds*, while we retain resentments for years. Pride constantly hides in a corner of our hearts, waiting, hoping to devour our fledgling insights. As soon as we forget our total dependence on God and think that in this particular area we'll have to protect ourselves, we sink like Peter walking on the water. We once again take up the shield of delusion and the sword of self-righteousness, blaming God for an imperfect world where we must fight to meet our needs.

Do Our Defects Define Us?

Confronted with this step, we also fear that we will lose our personalities, and as Bill W. says, become the hole in the donut. Step Six deepens our understanding of Step Three. We fear we will disappear if we give up our character defects/defenses. We are so identified with our defenses we feel there will be nothing left of us if we give them up. Of course, once again, we are listening to pride's lies. Grace reminds us God has never made and never will make anything, not even the downy feathers of a newly hatched duck, like anything else. God in his infinite creative power loves variety, and the more we trust God to continue to create us in his image, the more we are free to be individuals, and the more creative we become.

Gossip

When I assassinate others through gossip, I justify myself and my defects by showing someone else to be as low or lower than I am. Love covers sin; gossip uncovers it. Love diminishes sin; gossip multiplies it. Sarcasm does the same thing, but I use humor to disguise my motive. When I fully accept myself, completely justified through God's love, my tendency is to "cover" the sins of others rather than reveal them. I cover them with the grace and forgiveness I've received. When love says I must reveal the faults of others, I do so in love, not to please other people or to justify myself. If I ever reveal someone else's faults it is to encourage their spiritual growth, and I do so gently, with some confession of my own character defects. This is the ideal towards which I reach. Gossip is still one of my character defects, but I'm better than I was and not as good as I'm going to be.

Sex

We dress up our illicit sexual relationships, saying we're simply "getting our needs met." This may be true, but it is not a noble, God-given need we pursue. We may have a need to feel power over another person, instead of experiencing and enjoying the power that comes from God. We may be acting out of self-pity, thinking since we didn't receive the love we should have from our parents or from our spouse, we have the right to take it where we can find it, instead of looking to God to fill us with his limitless, unconditional love. Or we may be attempting to satisfy a need to see ourselves as attractive and desirable to others instead of acknowledging that our worth is affirmed by the Author of Love.

Resentment

Our resentments toward others are hard won and we feel sure we need to protect ourselves by nursing them; it keeps us on our toes. And remembering the sins of others keeps us from seeing our own. We don't want to believe that forgetting is a vital part of forgiving. If we have not forgotten, we have not forgiven. What if God said, "I'm going to forgive this, but I'm not going to forget it." We understand intuitively this can't be. No, God says he forgets our sins when he forgives, and our forgiveness should imitate his.

We know in our hearts that forgiveness must include forgetting; but our fear of future hurt, coupled with our aversion to seeing our own sins, prevents us from taking this step. The information in our brains can't be erased. But here we mean letting go of the feelings associated with the incident and refusing to continue to recall it for endless re-examination. We also need to forget the things for which we, ourselves, are forgiven. Interestingly, this may be the hardest for some of us. Pride makes us refuse to accept our own forgiveness; we don't want to allow God to have this kind of power over us. As long as our sins are so bad that God can't forgive them, we have power over him! But resentment sours our relationships with everyone and everything until we become ready to give up this character defect.

Anger

We feel we were weaklings most of our lives; we allowed others to push us around. We had finally begun to stand up for ourselves and vent our anger appropriately. Now we are told we must give up using anger as a defense and trust God to take care of us. We were enjoying our newfound power and were proud of our ability to get our needs met. We don't want God to defend us; we want others to know we are somebody and have rights. We don't realize that our fear can't be managed through our own resources. We've forgotten how powerless we really are and how vulnerable we are. We may be able to control the behavior of others to some degree through our anger, but we can never control their thoughts or feelings. We only isolate ourselves. Christ tells us not to contend with evil but to turn the other cheek (Matthew 5:38, 39), not because he likes evil, but that evil is far stronger than we are. When presented with lies, abuse, manipulations, selfishness, etc., on the part of others it is not "flesh" we contend with, but with the power of evil. Paul says in his letter to the Ephesians that the whole armor of God is necessary to defend us against evil and that thinking our anger is an effective weapon is an illusion.

Lying

We see dishonesty rewarded all around us. We probably even think we see those who are most dishonest receiving the promotions and prizes. We don't like being dishonest anymore than anyone else, but we're realists and do what we must to be rewarded in a hostile world. Yet what a price we pay for dishonesty. The price is low self-esteem, driving us to find esteem through the approval of others. We are unable to look to God for justification because we have no intention of obeying God by trusting him to meet our needs. Looking for esteem from others who have little or none themselves is a fruitless undertaking, but we are afraid to look to those who appear to have high self-esteem, since we're sure they would scorn us. We are really in a mess, doomed to go through life filled with anger and fear, sure we are worthless cowards, consumed with compromise.

The only answer to this dilemma is to trust God and see what happens. Really, we were wrong about several things. First, when we speak the truth in love wonderful things often happen rather than disastrous things. We have never before known how to speak the truth in love and so make it acceptable to others. We used truth as a weapon, not as a caress. Also, we blamed the duplicity in the world for our own lack of success. We claimed we had to compromise, to fight evil with evil in order to cover up our own incompetence and laziness. Now that we're in a right relationship with the Creator of the universe, our incompetence and laziness diminish; we find we're able to intuitively understand things which used to baffle us, and our vitality is almost boundless. We're amazed to find that we rise up as on eagle's wings; we run and are not tired!

Jane, with the help of her sponsor, was finally able to see the destructiveness of her relationships, and became entirely ready to have God remove her defects of character. She saw that the problem wasn't her infidelity to her husband; that was just a symptom of her refusal to trust God to meet her needs. Character defects are anti-Sacraments. They are outward and visible signs of an inward lack of trust in God.

Jerry, on the other hand, in spite of the concerned confrontation by others in his groups and his sponsor, was not able to see that he used these young people to bolster his own sagging ego and provide for his self-justification. People know when they are being used and they rebel or manipulate us in return. Doing what may be, the right thing for the wrong reason always backfires. In reality, Jerry encouraged the boys to act up, so he could appear to be martyr and saint. Jerry, as far as I know, never understood that self-justification is empty. We rest easy only when the true judge justifies us, whose judgment is always mercy and whose love is always unchanging.

Pride hasn't allowed John to recover. He even became a counselor for a time in a treatment program, but he only used his position to confirm to himself and others that he was special. He wouldn't go to 12 Step meetings. When asked why, he said he "didn't need to." The reality was he didn't want to associate himself with addicts. Every time he weakly attempted to do the steps, when he came to Step Six, he couldn't bring himself to give up the delusion that he had to be special, be good enough, be perfect. Down he would fall again, to the bottom of the first step; thinking he was certainly not powerless, certainly not an addict.

Becoming Our Own Friend

By working Step Six, we grow more aware that our character defects, our defenses, are the source of our difficulties. We understand that it isn't what others do which disturbs us, it is our own fear that our needs won't be met which is the source of our emotional distress. This is why we violated our values through dishonesty, gossip, and sexual misconduct. Now we have turned over our lives—physical, emotional and spiritual—to a loving God, from whom we get perfect justification. Since our defenses are superfluous, we become entirely ready to have God remove them.

Step Two and the following steps mark the beginning of a lifelong process that is never completed. The more we root out our defeating defenses and trust God, the freer we become to love ourselves. As we trust God we become our own best friends instead of our own worst enemies. Once we give up harming ourselves, we also give up perceiving others as dangerous. When we quit being our own enemies, we find we have no effective enemies at all.

Chapter Seven

I first met Clyde as an A.A. volunteer in the hospital when I was being treated for alcohol dependency. After I completed treatment and was going to meetings in the community, I began to realize Clyde was different from anyone I had met before. He came to every A.A. meeting and shared his experience, strength and hope just as the others did, but there was a difference in quality that could be felt. Even in silence, Clyde seemed to personify serenity. He was relaxed and cheerful. He showed real concern for others. When he spoke there was almost a song in his voice. He always talked of how driven he had once been to be good, to do this and that, to get this and that, but now he had "peace of mind." Others often talked about how they had lost everything through alcoholism but all these things had been restored. Clyde never talked about any benefits from the program except that now he could care about other people and that he had "peace of mind." I began to listen very carefully to Clyde, because what I longed for most was "peace of mind."

Step Seven — *Humbly asked Him to remove our shortcomings.*

There are many paradoxes in spirituality. We're told that whoever loses his life will save it; that to those who have, more will be added, while for those who have little, what they have will be taken away; and, to love our neighbors and forsake children, parents and spouses to follow Christ. Another paradox is that a twelve-step program is a completely selfish program whose goal is to open us to God's love and enable us to love self and others. God seems selfish; he neither can nor will relate to us in areas where we have put other gods before him. This is not out of selfishness; it is in order to honor our freedom. Love wants to be in direct relationship with us because it is that relationship that brings us the greatest joy. And, it is that relationship that makes all our other relationships peaceful and joyful. A twelve-step program is one in which we put aside our other gods in order to relate rightly to the true, living God.

As we progress through the steps, we become freer of the illusion that people (including ourselves), places and things can give us peace. Not willing to trust God, we had trusted the idols of family, home, career, status. Now awakening from our dreams and entering into the reality of our right relation to God, we understand that reality must come first. It is only through right relation with God that we get the peace and power to relate positively and unselfishly with the rest of creation. So the twelve-step program must come first.

Here I must cry, "DANGER, DANGER!" God's will for us is to become like him, to love his creation in a selfless, unconditional way. Too often I have seen those in a twelve-step program become obsessed with the enjoyment of the program to the exclusion of family and to the detriment of other relationships. The goal of the program is to enable us to love God, self *and others,* not to become exclusive or judgmental. If our relationships with others are not improving we have gotten off track. Some of the fruits of a twelve-step program are patience and gentleness toward others, *especially* our families. Being imperfect people; we will never find perfect balance on the razor's edge, but the more right the relationship with God, the more balance we achieve.

Bill W. says the "chief activator of our defects had been fear—primarily fear that we would lose something we already possessed or would fail to get something we demanded. Living upon a basis of unsatisfied demands, we were in a state of continual disturbance and frustration." In Step Seven we move from seeking what I want from God and others to asking what God wants for me.

Please notice that I ask what God wants *for* me, not *from* me. For most of my life I felt a dreadful, helpless guilt, thinking God, just like my family and others, was making demands on me I couldn't fulfill. I had no idea that God was *my* servant. Jesus says over and over and gives many examples of his servanthood toward us: He washes the feet of the disciples; cooks breakfast for them by the lake. He goes out of his way to heal those who ask him. He feeds thousands. God demonstrates again and again his servanthood toward Israel. Like Christ, he describes himself as a mother hen who wants to gather her babies under her wings. In Step Seven we trust God both to know and care for our needs, and to have the ability and willingness to provide for them. Christ said the Father knows what we need and will provide for our needs when we seek the kingdom first—when we agree with him in Love. We have been afraid we wouldn't get what we needed, and have based our perception of our need on our limited view rather than trusting God's omniscient point of view, omnipotence, and perfect love for us.

Humility provides another new insight; we are unable to remove our own character defects. We more fully understand that our power is the power to allow God to be God. We have the power of willful decision; God owns the rest. The greatest, but most fearsome gift we've received is the gift of will, the authority to decide. These are the areas in which we exercise our intelligence, our personalities and our power. We become willing to give up our defenses and trust God, making the decision to ask him to remove our defects. He does the work. Before, we struggled unsuccessfully to be good. Now we have peace, because we know it is God who removes our character defects. We were trying to use our willpower the wrong way. We hadn't noticed that no one is righteous but God, and that if we were to become righteous it must come from him.

So humility means trusting God the way chicks trust the mother hen, the way the little child trusts good parents. Without this level of trust we never enter the kingdom. Like the brother of the prodigal son, we remain angry and refuse to come to the party. Those who are still angry can't come into the joy of the kingdom. Those who are still angry and resentful can't attain "peace of mind."

The quality I saw in Clyde was humility. He trusted God more than anyone I have yet met. He trusted God for everything. He even trusted God to help others recover. This faith put the song in his voice. He knew he planted the seed, but God produced the germination and growth. Twelve step programs are programs of attraction rather than promotion. Those like Clyde provide the attraction. He had what I wanted. I listened when Clyde spoke. I remembered his words. Finally, when I became ready to turn my will and life over to God, I did the things I'd heard Clyde say to do. It works!

We understand that we are made righteous through God's righteousness. We no longer have to justify ourselves or dishonestly please others to gain self-esteem. We realize that it's from God that we get our capacity to feel and think, the energy to work and play. God tells us he clothes the lilies and feeds the birds, caring when a sparrow falls, and that we are of much more value to him than birds. He knows and cares about our needs. Trusting God, we move out of ourselves, toward others.

Chapter Eight

I used to see a friend as a kind of "comrade in arms," one who would support me in adversity, be loyal to me when I was wrong, see things my way and agree with me while sharing my likes and dislikes. Now I see others as fellow strugglers caught up in fear; always afraid they will lose something they have or not get something they think they need. Forgiveness is a natural outgrowth of trusting God. Resentment is the symptom (anti-sacrament) of fear. Forgiveness is the outward sign (sacrament) of grace. Increasing my love for myself through reconciliation with creation is the purpose of Step Eight.

Mary had spent her life taking care of others. First she cared for an ill mother. Later she took nursing training and had a successful career as professional care-taker. She was married to a man who was alcoholic and a compulsive gambler. He also had a sexual addiction and frequently visited prostitutes. They had two grown children. One child, the daughter, had "beaten" addiction to cocaine, and was now "only" using alcohol. The son was married, and fighting a civil war within. Part of him wanted to be a "good" husband, father and a good provider—not to be like his father—while another part, the physical part of him with the disease of chemical dependency, wanted to drink all night long, every night. As they were growing up, Mary had done everything she could to make life for her children appear normal, to not have them affected by the excesses of their father. Although suffering terrible fear and stifling anger, she had put on a good, brave face for her children, to try to immunize them from destruction. And she had risen to the top of her profession by continuing her education, working overtime, and working crazy shifts to make her family financially secure.

Jack was a "jolly" fat man. He was always joking and laughing at work, where he was a high-school principal. Jack had a wife who was also a carbohydrate craver, and as overweight as he was. One of his children was "chubby" while the other was still slim. Jack felt he was a good husband and father. He wasn't rich, but his family was comfortable. He helped the children with their school work and made sure they had almost straight A's. He sent them to camp and took them to concerts. He gave them piano and swimming lessons. He thought himself to be a good husband. He never criticized his wife although he felt she tended to over-dramatize things and was somewhat hypochondriacal. He had never criticized her weight, and it had never bothered him until he had a heart attack and became involved in Overeaters Anonymous.

Step Eight — *Made a list of all persons he had harmed, and became willing to make amends of them all.*

Why?

Why do we need to do this? We've listed, shared and asked to be relieved of our character defects. Why irritate old wounds we hope are healing? Let sleeping dogs lie.

Many of us, such as those in the above stories, feel we really have harmed no one but ourselves and see Step Eight as unnecessary since there is so little to include. Once again we find ourselves beset by denial. Step Eight is a vital step in our progress toward oneness with ourselves, creation and God. By working Step Eight we take another giant step out of illusion and into the light. Step Eight continues our progress, increasing healing humility and furthering peace of mind.

Forgiveness

Step Eight is really a three-part step. The first part is hidden, but as soon as we take pencil in hand we discover the need for this initial activity. The first part of this step is forgiveness. Earlier we talked about how God's forgiveness and forgetfulness were interdependent, intertwined, and that it must be so in our own minds and hearts as well if we are to reflect his image. Forgiveness coupled with forgetfulness is a hard concept and deserves more thought. As soon as we sit down to attempt Step Eight, we remember the sins of others, all the bad things everyone did to us, and this prevents us from doing our work. The thought of how others have harmed us keeps us from seeing the harm we've done them. By looking at the misbehavior of others we see our own defects as retaliatory, a logical, reasonable reaction to the offenses of others. If we're to be fully delivered of our delusions, we must first do the work of forgiving and forgetting.

By now, if we have done a fearless and thorough moral inventory of ourselves, our work of forgiveness and forgetting should not be too difficult. After uprooting and disclosing our most disreputable defects, we find defects in others more tolerable. Being justified by God, we feel less need to justify ourselves by exposing the sins of others. Forgiveness coupled with forgetfulness, however, is still not an easy process. Pride lurks in the shadows of our minds, telling us we may not want to continue this difficult, silly program, God really can't be trusted completely in this way, and our collection of wrongs done to us by others may come in handy in the future. Pride encourages us to keep alive, at least in a small way, the memory of every wrong thing anyone ever did to us.

To gain the promises of the program, however, we must put pride aside and continue with our new trust in God. God says we're forgiven exactly the way we forgive. As we forgive and forget our own sins, we become able to forgive and forget the sins of others. Pride tells us we must remember our own sins or the sins of others. Pride wants us to continue our hopeless attempts to justify ourselves instead of receiving God's justification. Pride wants to keep our defects and those of others before us. Love wants to hide the multitude of sins; Love wants to cover and forget our sins. It isn't Love who recalls our sins and those of others. We, as co-conspirators with pride, are the ones who retain sin. Love separates us from our defects and those of others as far as the east is from the west, hides them as if in the depths of the ocean, and wants us to do the same.

We usually want to retain some resentments more than others. In my case, there was a person who had used her job position to harm me knowingly and deeply to the point of preventing my recovery, which would have meant my death. I wanted to sue her in court. My lawyer assured me we would win the case, and winning would mean she would lose her job. I was sure I had the right, even the obligation to bring this person to task so she could never harm someone else the way she harmed me. I was sure this person was totally evil.

Unhappily, in spite of all my efforts and attendance at meetings, I was unable to stay dry from alcohol or gain mental and emotional sobriety, the quality Clyde had so abundantly and which I so desperately lacked. One evening after a meeting, I was talking about my proposed lawsuit with a man who knew my case well and whom I loved. He asked when I would let go of all that resentment and become sober. I was devastated. I had believed that if anyone would understand my feelings this man would; we had worked together and he knew the awful woman.

Now he was telling me my problem with this person was my fault. I cried. Then I realized he was right! I decided my life was more important than my court case or resentment. I had heard others in the program say you could rid yourself of resentment by praying for the offending parties. Distasteful as it was at first, I prayed for the woman for several weeks. Finally, realizing I wasn't that woman's judge—God was—I received the grace to forgive and forget. I dropped the suit, and that was really the beginning of the fulfillment of the promises for me.

Through forgiveness, we understand that those who harmed us were acting out of fear of unmet needs, just as we were. Grace allowed me to see how I had harmed the woman; how for years I had arrogantly abused her, calling her stupid, inviting her to envy me. I asked her to forgive me, and we were no longer enemies. When we allow God to be the judge, trusting God to defend us and meet our needs, we're able to forgive and forget.

Another List

The second part of the step requires us to make another list. Once again we put pencil to paper to demonstrate our willingness to allow the program to be our teacher. Here, I should focus on the common human tendency to want to alter this program for the better. Initially, most of us who begin this program find many flaws in it. As one who majored in English in college and aspired to write, I didn't like the language Bill W. used in the books. I thought it was stilted and outdated. Also, I thought there were too many steps; I thought several could be combined and that some were totally unnecessary. In meetings I heard old timers talk about how they and others had wanted to change the program and how many had tried. Of course they slipped directly back to Step One. We call this trying to find an easier, softer way, the wide way we've been on all along, the way of our will.

Pride balks at the thought that we must follow these particular Twelve Steps in just the way suggested. We find this an affront to our intelligence. We think there must surely be other routes to serenity. As Clyde would say to those who feel this way, "Go ahead and try another way if you want, and if you're successful let me know. My own experience is that of trying everything possible before becoming willing to take these particular steps in this particular way. Every other path, although it looked promising, led to fear and anger. I took these steps and received freedom and happiness. All I have is my own experience. You can come up this way or go another way. Either way I wish you well."

Making our list, we want to be as thorough as we were in Step Four. Just as in Step Four, if we consciously leave anyone off out of fear or resentment, we will not receive the benefits of the step. We need to go back in time to our earliest memories. It doesn't matter that those we've harmed may be unavailable to make amends to. At this point, we just make the list. It must be exhaustive, based on the insights we presently have. As with the other steps, in the future we will come back to Step Eight with heightened awareness and deeper understanding.

Bill W. tells us that those we harmed are those with whom our needs collided. He describes harm as physical, mental, emotional or spiritual damage done to others. The more obvious harms are easy to identify—if we've stolen from or physically hurt someone. More subtle harm may involve lies told to protect ourselves or others, but which robbed those we lied to of emotional security. Mary had unknowingly done her children profound emotional harm by lying and hiding her own feelings. Mary's dissembling to her children deprived them of emotional security just as much as their father's behavior. Recognizing how she, herself, had hurt her children seemed at first as if it would devastate her, but ultimately it enabled her to reach out to her children in love to ask their forgiveness.

Often we behave as Jack did, becoming accomplices in the harm others are doing to themselves in order to meet our own needs. Jack encouraged the carbohydrate/sugar addiction in his wife and child so he could feed his own addiction. He always made sure there was a generous supply of snacks and sweets at home and used every occasion to overeat them. When his children went away at camp he sent them large boxes of candy and carbohydrate snacks. He hid even from himself his secret joy over the fact that his wife was more overweight than he was.

He was appalled when he learned that his need to satisfy his addiction—his carbohydrate craving—was contributing to the same addiction in his spouse and at least one child. He saw their family disease, asked forgiveness and provided a model for recovery.

We probably were surprised to discover that anger is a character defect. We may be even more surprised to discover that we always harm those toward whom we are angry. Returning to the story of the prodigal son, the elder brother's anger deprives his younger brother of love and forgiveness, while the father, the one who was harmed, isn't angry at all. Where there is no anger there is no guilt. The father hadn't harmed the younger son, so was able to run out to meet him when he saw him coming far off. The father didn't wait to see if the son would apologize, thinking of punishment, looking for contrition. The father ran out to meet him. We need to include in our list all those persons we would be unwilling to speak to if we saw them on the street, anyone we would cross the street to avoid if we saw them coming.

It seems on the face of it that those who suffer from gross character defects and do obvious harm to others have an easier time with Step Eight than do those who do more subtle damage. This is not the case, however, because God is just. Hidden harm done to others is something we commonly share. As I came around the steps a third time, I realized I had never loved my family. I had claimed love, cried tears, and made sacrifices, but I never *loved* them. Everything I did for them was to meet my own needs and justify myself as a good parent of my children, a good child of my parents, and to disguise the fact that I drank too much and took too much Valium.

I didn't love, not because I was a "bad" person, but because I never had the capacity to love. I had seen the world as a hostile place where one had to fight to get ahead. I'd directed all my time and efforts toward meeting the family's financial needs with enough money left to satisfy my addiction, and to shoring up my sagging self-esteem. I wanted my children to wear nice clothes and go to a private school to show what a good parent I was. My only real concern for them was that they might turn out badly, misbehave publicly, and I would be exposed as the terrible parent I really was. If they did publicly misbehave, I wanted to be able to say, "I did my best, but what can one expect with the world the way it is today?" I never had the freedom and happiness required truly to love my children, and they knew it. As truly as an algebraic formula, we love others in direct relation to our trust in God—little trust, little love; no trust, no love; much trust, much love. My children were bitter not because I hadn't done things for them, but because I didn't love them. In a sense, this book is a living amends to them.

As Mary and Jack come around the spiral stairs, they will also pass this way, and understand that previously they had been unable to love.

Remember, when we get spiritual things wrong they are usually backwards. It is so here. God, who serves us and loves us unconditionally, wants us to serve and unconditionally love our children. We do the opposite. We treat them as our servants and conditionally love them. We make it appear that we're serving them, but this is an illusion we create to manipulate them into serving us—to get what we want and need. We play a horrible spiritual trick on them; we withhold love and make *them* feel guilty. Then we wonder what's wrong with them!

More Willingness

The third part of Step Eight involves a profound spiritual change; we becoming willing to make amends to everyone. Similar to Step Six, we don't yet make amends, but we become willing to. The courage to make amends requires amazing grace, the power of Love, and we first must become willing. God's grace in us can't become action until we become willing. We can conjure endless reasons why we can't or shouldn't make amends, and so we don't yet consider the hows. We're walking by faith, not by sight. Willingness is a decision based on faith.

The promise of this step, along with Step Nine, is the ability to enjoy the best possible relationship with every person we know. Loneliness was just a symptom of our inability to love. With these steps, loneliness ends. It is another step which we never finish, but it is vitally important for our spiritual growth that we begin.

Chapter Nine

In a twelve step program we learn to love ourselves. This means always doing what we want to do. If we truly love ourselves, we will always want what is good for us. Amazingly, what is good for us spiritually, emotionally and physically will also be good for everyone else. Always doing what we want doesn't mean always liking what we do. Many times a day I do things I don't like very much or may actively dislike, but the doing achieves a goal I want. Therefore doing them is doing what I want to do. So now I do what I want to do, go where I want to go, with people I want to be with.

Carol hurt her parents badly for many years because of her chemical dependency. She turned their later years, years that should have been a time for freedom and fun, into a nightmare of fear, worry and anger. Unable to live alone and support her addiction, she lived with them. Every night she became intoxicated, engaging in the wild, unpredictable, destructive, and dangerous behavior of chemical abuse. Most of her friends had abandoned her because of her chronic intoxication, but the few she had left also suffered from addiction and their behavior matched her own. Occasionally, she would go out driving. She had wrecks, she got DUI's, and she always called her father to bail her out and help with the damage. Her parents lived in terror. They were afraid to go anywhere, to visit friends or relatives, afraid to leave her alone. They were unable to have friends or relatives visit because of her unpredictable behavior. They were prisoners. Finally they died. Her dad died last, and near the end he pleaded with her to stop drinking because it worried him so. Shortly after his death she went into treatment and A.A.

Allen was a minister who was in a family program. He was the adult child of chemically dependent parents, and was married to a beautiful woman addicted to Valium. As the marriage relationship grew worse, Allen fell in love with a young woman he was counseling. They began an affair that lasted over a year. Allen's wife became suspicious when members of the congregation began remarking on how close Allen and his counselee appeared to be. Allen always denied any relationship other than a professional one.

Ben was an alcoholic attorney, now recovering in the program of A.A. During his years as a practicing alcoholic, his parents both died, and he was responsible for the estate. They had not left a will. In dispersing their belongings among the family, Ben literally stole a quantity of very valuable silver, which he sold to get himself out of some alcohol-related debt. The family never discovered his theft.

Step Nine — *Made direct amends to such people wherever possible, except when to do so would injure them or others.*

The Most Difficult Situation

Step Nine is another action step, and may be the hardest of the twelve. Clearly seeing and understanding the harm we've done others, coming face-to-face with them, acknowledging our wrongs and apologizing, and offering to restore their losses wherever possible requires a giant leap in humility and trust that God will sustain us in our efforts. The benefit is commensurate with the difficulty. After completing Step Nine we truly rejoice in knowledge of the power of God's grace and love. Step Nine is a sacrament, an outward and visable sign that we're really willing to love. Until we complete Step Nine, complete joy and peace elude us.

Reconciliation

For many years as a counselor, with what I thought was great wisdom, I would say that it took two people to make a relationship, meaning both carried responsibility for the flaws in the relationship. I believed a poor relationship was never the fault of only one person. Now I know I was wrong. It takes only *one* to make a relationship. In fact, natural law requires that we relate only as individuals to other individuals or things; that's how God designed relationship. My relationship with you is *my* relationship with you. Your relationship with me is *your* relationship with me. I can't directly participate in or influence your relationship with me nor can you directly participate in or influence my relationship with you. You may try to do the things that please me, but this by no means insures that I will be pleased since I bring all my history and experience from the time I was in my mother's womb into my interpretation of your actions. I may completely misinterpret what you do or say; and you can't anticipate, prevent or influence my interpretation. I may have another agenda that requires me to be displeased with you, so I pervert and twist your words or actions into something negative. I may be feeling badly for other reasons and find it convenient to blame you for my feelings. No matter how you try to please me, because I still feel badly, I may think you don't love or care for me. You can't directly affect my thoughts or mood. Whatever you do must be filtered through my senses, mind and soul; I put whatever interpretation on your words and action I feel fits.

This little-known fact wrecks the lives of the spouses and children of chemically dependent people. Those who are chemically dependent due to genetic predisposition are subject to feelings of anxiety, anger and depression. Having been taught, as most of us are, that people, places and things should make them happy, they expect their families to make them happy. The family has also been taught that spouses and children should make spouses and parents happy, so they feel low self-esteem when they are unable to please the chemically dependent person. *They rate their personal value relative to the happiness of a person with a metabolic disorder that causes the person to be depressed, angry and anxious.* It is clear that their defeat is as sure as the rising sun.

Once family members leave their chemically dependent relative through divorce or, in the case of children, by becoming adults, they often become attached to another dependent person in an attempt to "make them happy." They continue to hope to gain their own self-worth by helping someone, by making someone who is unhappy happy. It never occurs to them to have a relationship with someone who was happy and secure. In fact, if it had occurred to them they would find the thought unsettling. Their goal in relationships is to meet someone's need, make someone happy. Since their goal is an impossible one (making another person happy), they never engage in healthy relationships.

This apparent diversion was to explain why amends are always successful. Since my relationship is my own, and my own responsibility, and is independent of the response of others, I can love my enemies even if they prefer to remain my enemies. I now have perfect freedom in my relationships. If my children want to respond to my amends with forgiveness, that is truly blessed. If not, I can still maintain my loving relationship with them. The old saying, "No one can tell me who my friends are," will come true. My attitude toward others is no longer dependent on their attitude toward me. And knowing that God is my refuge and my sure defense, I don't have to fear them when I approach them to make amends. My new fearless, loving attitude toward those whom I've harmed becomes almost irresistible; some of those I hurt the most and feared the most are overjoyed to see the change in me and accept my amends gracefully.

Yets, there will be those who want to continue to be angry. They have found the harm you did to them useful for excusing their own bad behavior and rationalizing their own character defects. They will not give up anger that meets a personal need. These folks are as emotionally ill as you were. You feel sympathy for them, but you no longer need to fear them.

We often resist taking the ninth step because we're afraid to face the anger of those we've offended. Notice the word "afraid." We still fear seeing ourselves through the eyes of those we've harmed, we're still basing our self-image on the illusive praise and good will of others rather than on the reality of God's love. We ask for more humility, a deeper understanding of our right relationship to God as his children so we may give up this irrational fear and get on with our work of love.

Carol experienced forgiveness through working the fourth and fifth steps, but felt deep sadness over the awful harm she had done her parents. She now knew they had been enablers, helping her remain sick, but she also knew that they had no understanding of chemical dependency and acted out of selfless love for her. She was haunted by her inability to share her sobriety with them and ask their forgiveness. She talked with an A.A. friend, who told her others in the program recommended going to the grave and making amends to them there. At first, this seemed somewhat bizarre. Yet Carol was learning to listen to those who had found serenity. She went to the grave and made peace with her parents. Carol knew her parents weren't in the grave, that their spirits were with God, but her pilgrimage was a sacrament, an outward, visible sign confirming her inward and spiritual repentance. She needed an action to go with her thoughts and feelings to give them reality. This is the heart of amends making.

Allen avoided taking the ninth step concerning his infidelity. He rationalized that doing so would hurt both his wife and mistress. The peace of the program promised eluded him. One evening at a step meeting, he heard a fellow member talk of his own pride preventing him from making the amends necessary for peace of mind. Allen recognized himself in the mirror of his friend. It wasn't concern for others at all that kept him from his goal, it was plain old pride, once again dressed up, disguised as a noble motivation. He was ashamed to acknowledge his disloyalty and dishonesty.

He talked with this wife. She raged and increased her chemical consumption. Yet now that Allen was free from guilt he had the power to get treatment for his wife. He understood that his guilt had immobilized him in the relationship. He found that another benefit of the ninth step is receiving the power to work for the good of the beloved. He was also blessed with a new loving, moral power in his relationship with his children; they were beginning to experiment with chemicals and desperately needed a good, strong father.

Ben could see nothing but harm coming from amends he might make to his family over the stolen silver. He was now in a position to pay them back; that wasn't the problem. For many years his drinking had caused them to have a low opinion of him, and he was just beginning to earn their respect. Why shatter their improved image of him with revelations which wouldn't really benefit anyone? None of them needed the money and they had never known or even suspected he had robbed them.

Although he was being invited to family functions, Ben avoided them. He saw his family only when necessary and then felt uncomfortable, although they were very friendly to him. He was having trouble sleeping at night; he felt there was something he needed to do and couldn't remember what it was. He was having trouble concentrating at work, and his memory wasn't improving as fast as he thought it should. He felt depressed.

When Ben talked to his sponsor about his depression, the sponsor asked if there were anyone on his eighth step list to whom he had not made amends. Ben told the sponsor about his reluctance to admit his theft to his family, for their good as well as his own. The sponsor helped Ben see that his fear of the family's reaction wasn't based on real concern for them, but because he was still people-pleasing, still needed people's approval, still wasn't fully relying on God's approval for his self-worth. Ben saw that he had to make amends and let the chips fall. He talked to his family, made monetary restitution, and found they were overjoyed that he had made so much progress in recovery. They welcomed him into their lives even more than before. He reaped the promises of a new freedom and a new happiness, without fear of people and economic insecurity. He slept soundly and found life gratifying.

Does our newly found trust in God mean that we no longer need relationships? Of course not! But now we trust God to know this need and provide us with persons to love. God promises us he will supply us with family and friends, as well as meeting our physical needs. We no longer have to try desperately to manipulate others into meeting our need for relationship. We are free to love our neighbors and ourselves.

The Proof Is the Fruit

If we decide not to make amends to anyone on our list, the motivation must truly be loving or we will not reap the benefits the steps promise. The test is the fruit of the decision. If the fruit is peace, the decision was based on love. If the fruit is uneasiness, we are still motivated by fear, no matter how nicely it is dressed up, no matter how cleverly disguised.

This is a critical step. The completion of this step confirms our willingness to become at one with God, creation and ourselves.

Chapter Ten

We hate to see those we love suffer. When we love ourselves we do what we can to prevent or shorten our own suffering. When we are wrong, we suffer.

I am not a carpenter. One spring I decided it would be nice for us to raise baby ducks and chickens in our backyard on the river. I constructed a pen with chicken wire under the steps of my daughter's playhouse, went to the feed store and bought five ducklings and two chicks, and happily placed them in the pen. When my husband came home he said the dog would get in the pen and kill the animals. I said it wouldn't. He said it would. I said it wouldn't.

As I worked outside the next day I kept watch on the dog to be sure it couldn't get in the pen. At one point I became engrossed in the new garden I was planting and forgot to keep watch. A few minutes later I remembered, looked, and saw the dog running happily in the pen. But there was no other movement. He had done what he was bred to do. He had neatly broken the necks of all the animals. I was aghast, then I was angry that he killed the fowl, then I was angry that I hadn't protected them better, then I was angry that my husband had been right and I had been wrong. I was also ashamed to have to tell my daughter. She, by then, had come running up to see what was wrong. My pride was in total control and I had completely forgotten my twelve step program.

I told my daughter we would put these dead ones in the river for burial, get some more just like them, and her daddy would never notice the difference. I told her we wouldn't say anything if he didn't notice. We put them in the river, bought replacements, and I got some boards to nail around the bottom of the pen. I was appalled to see one carcass stuck in the river on a cypress stump and wouldn't float away. I was terrified my husband would see it, and even threw rocks and sticks at it to try to dislodge it. It stayed put, feathers gleaming in the sun.

Step Ten — *Continued to take personal inventory, and when we were wrong promptly admitted it.*

Pride Back, on the Attack

Step Ten is a two-part step, and we will examine the second part first. Pride, with our parents' and teachers' cooperation, tells us we should be perfect people. A terrible paradox in many families is the tendency for parents to withhold love when children are less than perfect (an activity which is very un-Godlike; evil is the absence of love), making their children feel guilty, making children feel it's their fault that the parents don't love them. (We violate our children twice with one stroke. We don't love them and then we make them feel guilty that we don't! Thanks be to God for mercy, for we could never truly amend such an awful crime.) So when we make what we see as a serious mistake, the four dark horsemen of pride, fear, anger and guilt rush to the defense. We should never make mistakes. We should be omnipotent and omniscient.

These, of course, are qualities of God, not human beings, and humility, if sought, returns us to right size. Humility reminds us we can't know everything, we can't anticipate the future, we don't know people fully, wholly, as God does, and we can't change much except ourselves—in other words, we often make mistakes. The program of Alcoholics Anonymous has another profoundly freeing little saying: I have a right to be wrong. Lifelong habits formed by our families and instructors and by our own desire to be God are hard to break, and when we are surprised or knocked off balance by making some personal error, they tend to leap into play. Defensive pride comes back in a rush. We lie, we try to hide our guilt, and blame others so we can pretend we are perfect people.

As you can see in my case, I not only lied, covered up and blamed others (the dog); I also taught my daughter a remarkable lesson in lying, covering up and blaming others. When my husband returned home he didn't notice the floating yellow body, nor did he notice the switch. Our secret was safe.

It seemed like such a little thing. The fowl didn't cost much to replace. The dog had been soundly chastised and I thought he would never bother another duck or chicken. The pen had been fortified to keep the animals safe. What my husband didn't know wouldn't hurt him. But peace of mind had vanished. I was ashamed of myself. Anger and resentment were my constant companions again. I was angry at myself for allowing the poor creatures to be killed, angry at my husband for knowing better than I what was bound to happen, angry at the dog for showing up my lack of omniscience—a quality my husband seemed to have in abundance. I resented my daughter's knowing I had taught her to do something I would punish her for if she had done it to me, and for seeing my shame.

It was terrible. Usually, I sleep like a baby. I couldn't go to sleep at all. My husband finally asked me what was wrong. I had been praying all the while for God to give me the grace to let go of pride and tell the truth. God did and I told my husband the truth. It wasn't easy, but after his sadness, he was understanding. I apologized to my daughter also, admitting that my example had been less than positive.

We almost never lie because of concern for another. Lies are almost always the result of fear that we will be hurt or that our pride will suffer, that we will be found to be not perfect. A human quality that can be very beneficial, the quality of shame, gets turned around 180 degrees, as all spiritual problems do, so that we are ashamed of being imperfect instead of being ashamed to lie. The shame we should rightly feel toward God is wrongly felt toward another human being.

Here is another 180 degree misuse of a spiritual quality, guilt. I feel guilty when I and/or others discover my imperfections, but I do not feel guilt (because I rationalize my behavior) when I act defensively out of fear, not trusting God. I'm far more afraid of making a mistake that reveals my creaturely limitations than I am of making a real, moral mistake. The worst thing that can happen is making a mistake reveals I'm not God.

Adam and Eve in the garden covered their bodies and hid because they were ashamed. They discovered they were not God; they were creatures. Ever since, we have been trying to deny that reality. Humanity's history is one of trying to dissolve limitations and gain control through magic, science and technology, to become omniscient and omnipotent. We say things are humiliating when we run into the wall of our creaturely limitations. If we are wrong and don't promptly admit it, we will promptly lie, cover up and blame others.

Love is Prompt to Heal

No matter how hard we try to dress up or disguise our character defects, we all have spiritual eyes by which we see them, and we feel guilty. This is a spiritual principle as absolute as the laws of thermodynamics in physics. Everyone knows it. The most isolated primitive in the bush knows it. The most powerful person of great wealth knows it. The most brilliant scientist knows it. The most depraved sinner knows it. God isn't without a witness to his law of love; it's written in everyone's innermost being. And when the law is violated, there are consequences.

The initial consequences may not be outward and visible, although they always become so, but there will be suffering of the soul—isolation, fear, anger, resentment, anxiety and depression. People who become willing to do a twelve step program are people who are tired of suffering and so have become willing to go to any lengths to stop hurting, even to remarkable lengths of admitting it promptly when they're wrong.

The twelve step program is pragmatic. Since we can't be God, it provides what we truly need. It provides us with the God of our understanding, whom we can trust and who loves us powerfully and unconditionally. The Twelve Steps make us feel good. Pride and deception make us feel bad. What a choice. We discover that promptly admitting we are wrong is really the easier, softer way; the way of self-seeking and fear is the harder, painful way.

Daily Inventory

The first part of this step advises us to take a daily personal inventory. Our inventory should be personal because, as Bill W. says, we never find peace by confessing the sins of others. Christ advises us to examine ourselves and not to judge others, that the judgment with which we judge others is the judgment we ourselves receive. Paul tells us that love covers sin rather than exposing it. We have no business taking another's inventory unless they ask us, and then we must speak the truth in *love*. Just as our fear of other people slipped away, our criticism of others must also slip away.

A daily personal inventory doesn't need to be and shouldn't be just an inventory of the wrongs we've done. We can joyfully inventory the times in our day when we trusted God and loved ourselves and our neighbor! Making this daily inventory we feel and see God's grace in our hearts and lives. We held our tongue when we wanted to gossip. We had the grace to give someone a real compliment. We enjoyed playing with our children or listening to our spouse's conversation. We moved past tolerance toward true love for our neighbors—whoever is nearby.

Living well, in peace with ourselves, creation and God, will become the norm, with anger an unpleasant surprise to be dealt with as soon as possible. The joy of our relationship with the creator and creation will become the norm rather than fleeting. In Step Ten we continue to grow in humility; the less we try to play God, the more God's spirit fills us. The more powerless we recognize ourselves to be, the more power God gives us by living in and through us. We recognize that we didn't speak the universe into existence out of nothing, we didn't cause the stuff of matter to dance and whirl and stick together with a power greater than that of the sun, but that the God who did love us as his children and shares his joy and power with us. God's shared power is always the power to love, since God is love. God even supplies the love with which we love him. And when we ask, he supplies the power we need to love ourselves enough to admit it when we are wrong.

Chapter Eleven

If I make billions of dollars, if the world becomes one political unit and I become its president, if millions flock to hear my words, if I sacrifice my life to save humanity; if any of these things or more happens and I don't love myself, I have nothing. God has little interest in what I do; he's infinitely interested in what I am. As another counselor says, "I'm a human being, not a human doing."

God makes each of us different. Through our differences, even through our disabilities, we can discover that the ground of our being is love. I'm made in God's likeness and God is love.

Joe was a drill instructor in the army. He was a real tough guy who bragged about his hard drinking, womanizing and motorcycle riding. He had a potato face that looked like it had been poorly dug, with multiple scars from biking accidents. The biking accidents drove him into treatment and A.A. Joe had some initial slips as most people do, but he accepted his condition and was making progress in the steps until he came to Step Eleven. He was a professional soldier without much formal education. The prayer part seemed doable, but the meditation part seemed effeminate and intellectual. Also, he was living in the barracks, as he was estranged from his wife, and he could imagine the hoots he'd get from the other GI's if he pulled out a Bible or some other meditation material to study. He figured he could skip over the meditation part and get on with the program.

Step Eleven — *Sought through prayer and meditation to improve our conscious contact with God, praying only for knowledge of His will for us and the power to carry that out.*

Tasting the joy of the love of God, we want to improve our conscious contact with him to broaden and deepen the relationship. We know that the only power we have apart from God is the power to decide whether to trust his will for us. We know that if we get off track the natural consequences are depression, fear, anger, self-pity and self-justification. Having experienced enough of that, we go to any lengths to continue to maintain and deepen our trust in God.

Prayer

Prayer and meditation may be something we haven't had much experience with. Our only experience with prayer may have been to ask God to do our will. If either of these is true, we have to begin from scratch. Paul tells us to pray without ceasing. This seems impossible and unnecessary. How and why would we pray without ceasing? Our minds run on incessantly. We are always in mental conversation with someone about something. Usually we are talking to ourselves. St. Paul knew that our minds are constantly active; he meant for us to be continuously conscious of God's presence.

Prayer is relationship to God with a mind open to listening as well as talking. Prayer is the conscious awareness that God is alive, and is with you always, everywhere. God is like an inner Siamese twin. Nothing can separate us from the presence of God. King David said there was nowhere he could go to escape from God. If he went down to hell, God was there also; there was nowhere in creation that he could go to hide from the presence of God.

Prayer is the acknowledgement of this constant presence. Always, in everything I do, I make a decision to do my will or God's will and there is nothing so small or ordinary that it escapes God's love and care. God's will is constant love. M. Scott Peck, M.D., in his book *The Road Less Traveled,* defines love as that which produces or enhances spiritual growth. Using this definition love can take many forms, and at times appear not loving at all! As our concept of love deepens, we discover it is not a sentimental feeling. Because of love we may allow a loved one to suffer the painful consequences of misdirected behavior in order to promote their spiritual growth. When we are motivated by a lack of trust in God, fear, anger and the need for self-justification are the natural results. This is true for every human being who is, was, or will be created. None of us can escape the constant love of God, and therefore we can't escape the constant judgment of ourselves by ourselves when we are unloving. So we become increasingly aware that God is in us, that love is his motivation in all things, and that he will, if asked, empower us to love our neighbors and ourselves in all we do. In prayer, we improve our conscious awareness of God's constant, loving, powerful presence.

Meditation

Prayer is something we can do always everywhere. Meditation is an activity that requires some degree of concentration. The concentration required, however, is not "hard thinking" on our part, it is concentrating on opening our minds to God so we can receive insights beyond the range of our limited abilities. Meditation is most successful when there is a concept or idea or question on which we focus, asking God to deepen our understanding. God's love is perfect freedom; he won't walk over our brains with hob-nailed boots. He won't say in a loud voice, "I'm God, and this is what I have to say." He speaks in a "still, small voice" which is easy to miss or ignore. Our conscious contact with God in prayer or meditation is a two-way street, but we initiate contact. God never gives advice unasked. He is always present, but won't make himself known unless invited; this is the awful freedom God gives us. In meditation we go to God with some specific problem or question.

Joe was stuck. He seemed to be making no progress, but had lots of questions. He asked his sponsor endless questions, but his sponsor's only response was to read the "Big Book" (*Alcoholic Anonymous*) and go to meetings. This made Joe furious. He contemplated firing his sponsor for refusing to answer questions, but because Joe respected his sponsor, he did as directed, and began to study the book. Through this study, he lost his fear of what the other GI's thought were appropriate pursuits, and openly began to study the biblical passages recommended by A.A.'s original members.

Through meditation, Joe's understanding of himself deepened and his fear dissolved. He began to relate to his family in new ways, and finally reconciled with them. I had the opportunity to follow Joe's progress for many years, and when I last saw him, his recovery was excellent. He had received promotions up to the rank of sergeant major, and was sponsoring others.

The biblical materials Joe used for meditation were Matthew 6:25-34, especially, and the Sermon on the Mount, Matthew 5 and 6 and 7:1-29. Also in Matthew 6 he found the Lord's Prayer, which in itself is a wonderful tool for meditation. Almost every word can be contemplated. The founding fathers and mothers of A.A. recommended the Letter of James as well, and Joe attributed much of his spiritual progress to the study of this text.

Meditations on the Lord's Prayer might begin by contemplating the word "our." Christ didn't suggest that we pray "*my* father," but "*our* Father." We might ask God to assist us in understanding what he meant when he said "our." Here we might relax and allow our minds to rest, open to instruction. We may understand that God wants us to recognize him as Father of all. We begin to see the word "our" as being all-inclusive, realizing our true relationship with the rest of humanity through a common Father. The question put to Jesus, "Who is my neighbor?" takes on a new meaning, so that I realize my neighbor is whoever is nearby, and whoever is nearby is my brother or sister.

On a deeper level, I may receive the insight that all living cells divide, carrying some of the original cell into the new cells; therefore, bio-chemically I am one with all of life, beginning with the first divided cell. Thus I broaden my understanding of the father-hood of God. As I continue to contemplate the word "our," I see all creation as kin. As my meditation on the word develops, I see that loving my neighbor as myself is really a natural law rather than something I should try and do; I always value the neighbor with exactly the value I have for myself. If I see myself as a beloved child of God, I also see my neighbor as such. If I see myself as of little value, having to struggle in a hostile world to protect my rights and meet my needs, I see my neighbor as having little value as well, and as a competitor in the struggle. If I see myself alone in a hostile universe, I have no concern for the environment. If I see myself as a child of the loving God who is also Father to the rest of creation, I will love creation and treat it as I do myself. I will become at one with all creation.

A meditation I found helpful was triggered by a

talk with a real estate agent who was selling our property, and who was also in a twelve step program. When we had what I felt to be difficult decisions to make, he remarked that I shouldn't take things too seriously. He said, "For me, when I get serious, I get close to death. It means I've lost touch with reality. Nothing is serious." I thought about what he said, and remembered a passage in the eighth chapter of Paul's letter to the Romans, a passage I had used in the burial of my parents, the same passage I mentioned in Step Three. Part of it goes, "For I am convinced that there is nothing in death or life, in the realm of spirits or superhuman powers, in the world as it is or in the world as it shall be, in all the forces of the universe, in heights or depths—nothing in all creation that can separate us from the love of God in Christ Jesus our Lord." Meditation on this passage brought understanding of what he meant. The only thing that really mattered was God's love for me, and nothing in all creation could separate me from it; therefore, nothing else was serious!

Other biblical passages I found important and helpful in my own recovery were those near the end of the book of Job. I have always been something of a know-it-all, relying heavily on my intellectual abilities and lording it over those less informed or less mentally agile. My husband once commented my tongue should be registered as a deadly weapon! An open mind was alien to me, although I would have protested mightily that mine was the most open of minds. I had seen more than my share of misery, not only my own but that of others. I spent years working with the poor at the Welfare Department. I worked with the elderly mentally ill at a veterans' hospital. As an addiction counselor, I witnessed the tragedy of chemical dependency as well as spouse and child physical and sexual abuse. I had seen the worst of what people do to people and what—I thought—God either does or allows to be done to people, and I was God's critic.

How, I asked, could a loving God allow all this evil and suffering? I decided God was unloving, or cruel, or careless, or crazy or had wound up the universe, let it go and left. When necessity (a matter of life or death) forced me to open my mind and talk of Step Two, I realized that part of my own arrogance, my own craziness was thinking I knew what was good and what was evil, and could be God's judge. This was also Job's experience, which he sums up in the 42nd chapter: "Then Job answered the Lord: 'I know that thou canst do all things, and that no purpose is beyond thee. But I have spoken of great things which I have not understood. Things too wonderful for me to know. I knew of thee then only by report, but now I see thee with my own eyes. Therefore I melt away; I repent in dust and ashes'" (New English Bible). Job had thought himself a good man and believed he understood the difference between good and evil. When he "sees" God and is confronted with this real relationship to the creator of the universe he despises his intellect, sees it as nothing, and repents of his pride.

Although some degree of quiet and concentration is needed for meditation—you can't meditate while conversing or listening to someone talk—you can meditate while doing activities that are automatic and require minimal concentration. Driving on a lonely road, cleaning house, gardening, jogging or walking all offer opportunities for meditation. Often we think meditation requires great effort on our part. It only requires a question and a listening heart. We don't need to sit in the lotus position or stand on our heads. We can listen to God as easily as we can listen to our spouse or our children. All we need is quiet and a pure heart—an honest desire to have God clarify a question and willingness to accept the answer.

What makes meditation so difficult is not God's unwillingness to answer; it's our unwillingness to hear God's answer. In other words, we talk to ourselves. Have you ever had someone ask your advice or opinion on a matter that was troubling him, then when you gave it, he rejected it? This person wasn't looking for advice or clarification, but for confirmation of his own answer. He'll probably ask other people's advice until he finds someone who agrees with him. Having the willingness to accept God's advice and opinion takes great humility. God promises us that if we ask for his opinion we will receive it, but it must be his opinion we want, not a reflection of our own!

The openness required in meditation consists in not holding on to preconceived ideas. In meditation, I let go of my old ideas and ask what God has to say.

Meditation doesn't so much require emptying the mind through mental tricks as it does letting go of old thought patterns and opening the mind to new ideas and points of view from God. God's wisdom is seldom conventional. In meditation we ask in openness with willingness to accept what God has to say. If God tells us to love our enemies, not to resist evil, to turn the other cheek, to forgive those who hurt us, that our anger doesn't work with God's righteousness, to give up anxiety and fear of economic insecurity because he assures us opportunities to get everything we need, we must be willing to accept what he says and do it. Meditation doesn't work for people who aren't willing to accept God's answers.

Thy Will Be Done

This brings us to the next part of the step, praying only for knowledge of His will for us and the power to carry it out. Humility is understanding who God is and who we are. As humility increases, we see more clearly that we do not and have never known what was good for us in reference to the particular. Several years ago, I had a very good job in Augusta, Georgia, home of the Masters' Golf Tournament, and one of the loveliest cities on the planet in springtime. My children and grandchildren lived there. I had a lovely house with a pool in a nice neighborhood. I had all my A.A. friends. I had my church, and I loved my priest. I was sober for the first time in my life, and was truly happy for the first time in my life. One evening, my husband came home from his job as prison chaplain, and told me he had been called to serve at Parchman Prison in the North Mississippi Delta. I couldn't believe it. This would turn my world upside-down! I'd have to leave my children and grandchildren and job and house and A.A. friends and church and job. I couldn't even find Parchman on the map! I guess you get the picture. I was angry. I was terrified. Finally, I accepted God's will. We moved. The result was nothing but blessing after blessing, opportunity after opportunity. Because we moved, I was able to do things I would have never been able to do in Augusta. And while the distance between my daughter and grandchildren has been painful, they spend lovely, carefree summers here. God even provided my grandsons with two boys their age across the street, with whom they've formed what will be life-long friendships. Their days on the banks of the Sunflower River with their friends will be days they won't forget. If I had stayed in Augusta, I'd just be one more older relative in a gaggle of extended family members, nothing special at all.

We know trust in God brings us peace, freedom and joy. We have learned that trusting our own will is usually disastrous when our will isn't merged with God's. Not being omniscient, we have trouble discerning from day to day what action will increase our happiness—our trust in God—and what action might diminish it. We notice that often adversity, the thing we prayed to avoid, is exactly the thing that increased our trust and made us happier. Happiness and freedom are wholly based on our relationship to God; we want to seek whatever will deepen that relationship. Since with our limited vision we don't know what to pray for, we trust God to know what we need, and pray only for knowledge of his will for us and the power to carry it out.

Frequently we are tempted to pray for specifics for others, especially when those we love are suffering. We want them to be happy and comfortable, certainly not in pain. We forget that happiness for them means their own relationship with God. In order to discover that people, places and things don't satisfy, they must go through the same painful processes we went through. To have a spiritual awakening, they, too, have to discover that temporal things are ultimately unsatisfying. The illness that brings them close to death, the loss of family or income, the disability they suffer may bring them into their own relationships with God, may bring them the ultimate joy, their eternal happiness.

We don't pray for adversity for those we love, we pray for them "Thy will be done," because God's will for them is always love, and God loves them more that we do. And we pray that they may be delivered from evil. "Evil" includes the delusion that anyone or anything besides trust in God will satisfy human need. This doesn't mean that we shouldn't help others, if we can, when this help doesn't relieve a natural negative consequence of their behavior. God acts through adversity to get into relationship with people, and only he knows what and how much adversity this requires.

Pursuing these steps, we discovered God is alive, and we have a personal, direct relationship with him. Our parents may have told us things about God, or perhaps we heard about God in church, or we may have read things about him. Like Job, in the past we had only heard, now we KNOW. We have conscious contact with God; we can discern directly his will for us. However, there is a danger. Bill W. points out that people with this experience can expound more arrogant nonsense, believing that "it was what God told them," than under any other guise. This is why we use tools for meditation. We need anchors so that we won't run off directionless. If we think we hear "God" tell us to do something that doesn't increase our trust in him or our love for our neighbors or ourselves, what we hear is not God's voice. God tells me what he wants me to know anytime I'm willing to listen and do his will.

As our humility grows through the practice of these steps, we continually deepen our understanding of our (and the universe's) total dependence on God; his spirit is the glue of the particles in the atoms of which our bodies are made, and gives them the power to dance. We didn't create our intelligence or knit together the cells of our muscles. And while we may use our God-given intelligence and muscles to plant the seeds, we don't cause the germination or the growth in the plants we eat. We know it is by God and in God that we live and move and have our being.

Chapter Twelve

When Pilate questioned Jesus, he asked, "What is truth?" Cynics also ask, what is love? This is always a cynical question since everyone knows what love is. For the sake of argument, let's define it, starting with what it isn't. Love isn't needing or wanting persons, places, or things. Real love casts out fear, and fear always accompanies need and want. Paul tells us love is patient and kind, not jealous or boastful, not arrogant or rude, doesn't insist on its own way, is not irritable or resentful, does not rejoice in wrong but rejoices in right, and never ends.

Jim came into the 12 step program for an eating disorder. He was over one hundred pounds overweight and was becoming diabetic. He had many physical complaints including rheumatoid arthritis and a sleep disorder caused by his excessive weight. Jim had seen many medical doctors, psychiatrists and counselors with only temporary relief. He tried endless diets with the same result. He believed his eating disorder was due to his history; as a child, he was sexually abused by his alcoholic step-father. His mother was also alcoholic. He had been a lonely, only child who because of his shame over his family talked to no one.

As an adult, he married an alcoholic. He physically and emotionally abused his children, although at the time he thought he was "doing the right thing." Jim had been in counseling for years. He tried therapist after therapist. But it didn't work. His case appeared hopeless to himself and his counselors. He presented so many problems, both physical and emotional, that his therapists eventually despaired of offering him any lasting help and, in fact, began to hate to see him coming. They all terminated treatment with goals not met. Then his wife became so ill she was forced into treatment. Attending the family therapy program, Jim learned his overeating was a form of addiction, and went to overeaters anonymous. Working the twelve steps, Jim became aware he had always presented his problems in such a way as to defeat every therapeutic intervention. He avoided taking any personal responsibility by blaming his family, society and God for all his difficulties. Those in the twelve-step program weren't interested in hearing what others had done to him; they were interested only in whether he was willing to work the steps. With no hope of finding another way to relieve his pain and regain his health, he became willing and began the process of recovery. Opening his mind, Jim saw that his mother and stepfather had exercised their God-given freedom to love or not to love. They were free and accountable, but so was he. He made the decision to accept Love and to love.

Ann had been in A.A. for two years, and "loved the fellowship." She was free from alcohol, but her relationships were awry, which mystified her. She was very involved in the program; she chaired meetings, was on committees, sponsored newcomers, and spent lots of time volunteering at the A.A. clubhouse. Ann entered counseling because of the pain in her relationship with her husband and children. She was basically estranged from them, although they lived in the same house. She was desperately lonely and was becoming sexually involved with one of the men in the program.

Step Twelve — *Having had a spiritual awakening as the result of these steps, we tried to carry this message to others [here A.A. says "alcoholics"] and practice these principles in all our affairs.*

Our "spiritual awakening" is awakening to the fact that God, who is all-powerful, all-knowing, all-seeing and all-loving, loves us as his own children, and nothing in all creation can separate us from that love.

This understanding brings fulfillment of the promises; we know a new freedom and a new happiness. We no longer regret the past. We have peace of mind. Self-pity disappears. We lose interest in getting our needs met and self-seeking slips away; we're interested in other people. Our whole attitude has changed. We no longer fear people or economic insecurity. We intuitively know how to handle problems that used to baffle us. We realize God is acting in our lives and accomplishing what we could not.

As the promises come true for us, our spiritual

awakening ripens. The more we trust God, the more we can trust him with! The more we trust God, the more we understand that it was he all along who sustained us even while we fought against him. We see that it was our own fearful and willful struggles that prevented us from seeing that we had what we needed all along—the One who is omnipotent, omniscient and eternal, loving, defending, and justifying us. Bill W. put it most beautifully in the book *Alcoholics Anonymous* when he said, "This great experience that released me from the bondage of hatred and replaced it with love is really just another affirmation of the truth I know: *I get everything I need in Alcoholics Anonymous [through the Twelve Steps]— everything I need I get—and when I get what I need I invariably find that it was just what I wanted all the time.*"

The more often I circle back to Step One with clearer vision, the more I enter into reality, the more completely I understand that I have no power at all except that of decision. I see profoundly I have done nothing that wasn't sustained by the power of God. I realize I didn't call myself into existence; I'm not in control of my biochemistry and don't provide the circuitry of nerve cells which give me the ability to think and comprehend. I see that I didn't arrange the opportunities I've been given to do work and relate to others. There's an old story of a farmer who, when someone mentioned to him how wonderful God was to provide him with such a beautiful farm, replied that they should have seen it when God had it by himself. Amusing, but the deeper truth is the farmer received from God his being, his muscle and brain power to do the work as well as the many opportunities which made purchase of the land, seeds and equipment possible. I know I'm powerless to do anything apart from God, but that doesn't mean I'm worthless. I'm God's child, and of enormous value. For God, because of who he is, each one of us is like his only child!

As we come around again to Step Two we more profoundly know we can trust God to meet our needs and orient us to reality. Again, the more we trust God, the more we believe we can trust God. The more we trust God, the more humility we have, the more we clearly see ourselves in relationship to God. We grow toward becoming human *beings* rather than human *doings*. As we are restored to sanity, or attain sanity for the first time, we understand "the reason we're here" is not to *do* anything, but to *be* in loving relationship with God. Once we are in right relationship with God we are free to love ourselves, our neighbors, the rest of creation, and even our enemies.

As we more fully trust God, each time we come around again to Step Three we find another facet of our lives we can turn over to God's will. Each time we re-take the third step, our deepening trust uncovers areas where we had wanted to maintain control in case God couldn't or wouldn't give us what we wanted. In the third step we exercise our decision-making power, the awesome, fearful power that God granted the angels and us, and with which he will not interfere. Making the decision required in Step

Three, we understand we can hold nothing in reserve. To receive the benefits of the third step we can leave no areas in our lives where we are consciously saying "no" to God. We must become willing to forgive those for whom we hold resentments, understanding we can do so only through his help, to give up attachments that are harmful to us, to turn over remaining addictions.

The decision of Step Three means trusting God to defend us, giving up fighting and defending ourselves. We no longer see the world as hostile, where we must struggle to survive; we see God's love reflected in creation, offering an environment that provides challenges and opportunities to deepen our trust and exercise our individual creativity. Every adversary presents the possibility of "thy will be done." In every threat, God asks if we trust him. We make Step Three's decision every day in everything we do. And as we grow, the more beautiful, interesting, exciting and meaningful all creation becomes.

As our attitude changes and we find it more profitable to trust God than ourselves, and we discover more old character defects we had unconsciously kept to provide for our defense and justification, we will want to take another fourth step. We may see that we deprived our families of love while we struggled to meet our needs, and understand this was as serious as any physical damage we may have done. We may be appalled at the anger with which we bombarded them to frighten them into doing our will, or at the passive games we played to make them feel guilty so they would meet our needs. We see that our protestations of love were really manipulation mechanisms to assure us of emotional support and provide self-justification.

Once these new character defects are uncovered, we rush to complete the next three steps in order to accept God's forgiveness, so we can make amends and become one with our fellows.

As we do Steps Eight and Nine again, facing these steps more realistically, we may become saddened when we see how much harm we have done to our families, especially our children. If we talk to our sponsor or partner in working the steps, we may be reminded that we were not the only person in the lives of the people we've harmed. God isn't without a witness. When we weren't able to reflect the love of God for our children, someone did.

Some damage was probably done, and our children may carry our genetic coding for chemical dependency, anxiety, or depression. As our children grow up, we frequently see them sinking into the same illnesses we suffered. At this point, we may benefit from doing the first three steps as they are done in Alanon, A.A.'s family program. They go like this: Admitted I was powerless over (person's name), and her/his life is unmanageable. Came to believe a power greater than myself could restore (person's name) to sanity. Made a decision to turn (person's name) will and life over to the God of my understanding. We don't need to bother with "survivor's guilt." God is in a private, intimate struggle with each individual; every person has the same awful power of decision we possess. God never allows anyone to become so disordered that this simple decision can't be made. Although occasionally therapists and others may facilitate a healing environment, God alone heals and can do so directly without any help from us. The only requirement is the willingness of the individual, and healing is solely between the person and God.

With greater trust in God, our ability to do Step Ten increases. We learn to speak the truth in love, where before we either spoke the truth without love, in order to justify ourselves and put ourselves in a higher position relative to the other person, or we didn't speak the truth, in order to people-please. Now that God provides our justification and meets our emotional needs, we are free to see when we slip into old habits of acting or reacting defensively, and promptly admit it to the person we harmed.

As our spiritual awakening deepens and our spiritual growth increases through Step Eleven, we find, as an old prayer says, that God is doing for us "better things than we can desire or pray for." We no longer look for the gift; the Giver is the greatest gift. We find the promise of the gift of the Holy Spirit of far greater value than "much fine gold." God's love for us fully meets our emotional needs in the perfect way the love we sought from others never could. And now that we know our needs are fully met, we are free and empowered to love others. We have truly been "looking for love in all the wrong faces, looking for love in all the wrong places." And we realize others couldn't meet our need for love because they were doing the same thing—looking to us to meet their need for love. Once we experience God's perfect, never-ending love, we know that what really matters isn't at all whether others love us, it's whether we love others. Being in a loving relationship with God, I'm free to love even my enemies. Being loved by others is still a blessing, but it isn't necessary in order for me to love them. I'm free to love anyone and everyone because God loves me!

Jim worked the steps, and started to practice these principles in all his affairs. He carried the message to others not only through his words, but in his life. This is what the apostle James means in his biblical letter, telling us to be doers, not hearers only. In A.A. terms, don't talk the talk if you can't walk the walk. If we practice these principles it will be obvious in our lives; our verbal message will be secondary. Everyone who knew Jim saw the transformation—the miracle. He was happy and peaceful, and people wanted to know how he got that way. His children were amazed. First they scoffed, expecting him to return to his old self. Then they resented his happiness while they still suffered. When I last saw Jim, one child had entered the Adult Children of Alcoholics program and was happily working the steps.

For Ann, things didn't go well. In spite of remaining in the fellowship of A.A., she did not, while I knew her, become willing to take the steps. She continued to try to manage the lives of her family, and finally drove them off with her constant complaints over their unwillingness to behave the way she wanted them to. Inside the fellowship, she gossiped and criticized others. People lost trust in her and left her sponsorship. Ann was like the people Christ described as tombs, whitewashed outside but dead inside. The program won't work unless we work the program. The promises are never fulfilled until we take the steps. Talking the talk without walking the walk is fruitless. We can never possess God's spirit and power without trusting God's will.

Working the steps we find a new freedom and a new happiness. There is no greater happiness and freedom than that found through discovering that the all-powerful, all-knowing, eternal Creator of the universe calls you into a direct, loving relationship with him as his very own child, to whom he will give the loving power of the Holy Spirit. Through God's love we really do become new creatures, no longer fear's slaves, in bondage to need. Knowing we are God's children, our healthy love for ourselves becomes perfected and is reflected in our love for others and for all creation. We know the peace that passes understanding.

As we practice these principles we reach out in love to our fellows, glad for any opportunity to talk about the miracle of God's power and love in our lives as a result of the twelve steps. We aren't ashamed to share our experience, strength and hope with others. Trusting God no longer seems a weakness; it's our greatest asset. As we reach out in love, we remember that God heals only when the individual is willing; we can take personal responsibility for no one's recovery.

Moving through the program of A.A., I often hear that A.A. doesn't really stand for Alcoholics Anonymous, it stands for Attitude Alteration. I'm told that through working the steps everything stays the same, but everything is different. For me this was true. Before I began working the steps, I felt hopeless, I felt everyone was against me, I felt no one understood me, I felt no one really loved me, I was filled with resentment and guilt. By the time I was halfway through the steps, I believed God loved me, and gave up my resentments and guilt. I no longer sought self-justification and I was beginning to experience the God-given ability to love myself and others. Nothing had changed; I had the same family, the same job, the same house, the same friends and enemies. Yet everything was different. And miracle of miracles, as I changed my attitude, the attitudes of many of those around me changed. Those who were enemies began to trust me. Many who were angry with me forgave me. Those who had been turned off by my defensive arrogance began to be attracted to me. Those who had run from me began to approach me. Most important, my attitude was thankfulness for God's calling me into existence and loving me. This gratitude produced the freedom and happiness I had always sought.

So, if you will, come along on this walk into God's kingdom of love, acceptance and forgiveness, and be transformed into his image through the power of his Spirit. Expect miracles!

Anger

Anger is so misunderstood and mishandled in our society I feel it will be helpful to spend some time talking about it.

Anger *is* a deadly sin. It kills the body as well as the soul. Studies have taken apart the characteristics of the type A personality, the hard driver, "workaholic" type who had seemed disposed to cardiovascular problems, and found hostility was the major causative factor. It is not "stress" in general that increases cholesterol and the probability of having cardiovascular disease, it is anger.

Conventional wisdom tells us anger is "a normal, healthy reaction" that empowers and energizes us to get our needs met. When faced with our assertiveness/aggression, others may acquiesce and do what we want, but we pay a precious price for getting our way. My experience with anger, my own and that of others, is that it blinds us and causes us to make mistakes. Think of soldiers and boxers. The advice they always get is to keep a cool head, knowing that the energizing benefits of anger are outweighed by the mental confusion it produces. If brute force, the battering ram of will, is all that's called for in a situation, perhaps anger might be of some benefit, but there are other driving emotions which can energize and which have far less damaging effects.

We dress anger up, disguising it as righteousness, fooling ourselves into not realizing it is a symptom of the most basic character defect. Anger is always a symptom of fear. Whenever we feel anger, it is nothing but the biochemistry of fear, clothed in more acceptable garb. Even what seems to be the most altruistic and righteous anger, anger felt when someone else is hurt or mistreated, is fear aroused because we are powerless to control or correct the situation. Fear is what we get when we face our powerlessness and don't yet trust God. This anger may move us to alert others to the problem, arouse their fear, and thereby gather social power to change the situation, but love could do the same thing better. Love has the stronger motivating power, clearer vision, and is healthy. Whenever we feel anger, it is always about control; we realize we aren't omnipotent, we do not have God's power. Reality breaks through our pride, and fear and anger result. Only the One who is righteous has the right to righteous anger.

Often we become angry (fearful) when we feel people don't love us or care about us as they should. We take personally their not seeming to find us worthy of their love and concern. Most often they aren't yet capable of caring love. *They* need someone to show *them* unconditional love, and they become angry when this need isn't met. We were all in need, asking from each other the perfect love we don't have to give. Often we made motions towards others which appeared loving and giving, but the effort didn't represent the true unconditional love of God, and was made in order to get them to love us in return. People weren't fooled into thinking that we "loved" them. They knew we were giving to get.

So as the drama plays around full-circle, perhaps we weren't worthy of other's love and concern, since it was out of selfishness that our loving gestures were made. When we felt people hadn't treated us fairly, we became angry and blamed them for our unhappiness, but our transaction was deceptive—we tried to deceive them by pretending our gesture was loving when in reality it was conditional, we were "loving" in order to get love in return.

Everyone knows real love can't be conditional; it can't be used as a bargaining chip. Love is a commitment, not a contract. Love loves forever, not only as long as you love me. Yet, we were not totally at fault. We were truly looking for love. The problem is that we were looking in the wrong place. People can't love until they receive God's love by opening their minds and trusting. So, this means there are very few people who are truly capable of love. Our family and friends don't fail to give us the love we need because we are unworthy or because they are unwilling. They haven't loved us because they were incapable. Only God can give us the unconditional love we need and empower us to love others unconditionally. When we trust God to meet our emotional needs and fill us with his loving Spirit we become able to love for the first time.

Bill W. tells us in the book "*The Twelve Steps and Twelve Traditions,*" that when we are tossed by the emotions of fear, anger, resentment and anxiety it is either because we haven't stirred ourselves to ask God's help to make the personal changes necessary to gain peace, or it is because we have not been willing to accept life on life's terms. We haven't yet acquired a right relationship with God. Like Job, we are still judging God, thinking we know better what is good for us, and how the universe should run. Anger is always a symptom of fear. Anxiety is a symptom of fear. And fear is a result of our prideful desire to run the show, thinking we know better than God.

So all problems are spiritual problems, and really all problems are one problem. In the story of Mary and Martha, where Mary was sitting and listening to Christ while Martha worked to get the dinner ready, we are told that Martha complained in anger and anxiety to Christ about Mary's not helping. Christ replied that Martha was worried and anxious about *many* things while only *one* was important, and Mary had chosen that one. God asks one question: "Will you trust me?" then leaves the decision up to us, guaranteeing our freedom. Living in God's will, living in love, is always perfect freedom. If God's power were manifested outside of mystery, we would have no choice. The visibility of God's power would compel our trust and there would be no question, no freedom, no independent decision. God's greatest creation is a creature whose will is independent. We are terribly free to say either "yes" or "no." God asks, "Will you trust me?" If we say "yes," the promises are fulfilled. If we say "no," our reward is anger, anxiety and resentment. To insure our freedom, to be sure we aren't overpowered by the Infinite Power, God hides, and this means our "yes" requires a leap of faith.

Trusting God, there is no need for anger. As the "Big Book" says, "We have stopped fighting anybody or anything." We believe God is sovereign and nothing happens which he doesn't allow and which he will not ultimately work out for our good. As the Psalmist says, "The Lord is my refuge and my sure defense, and he will be my savior."

Journey For Two
(or more)

One of the old sayings of A.A. is that you must do it yourself, but you can't do it alone. Trying to work these steps alone is only slightly better than not working them at all. We aren't equipped to see through our own delusions and rationalizations; if we were we wouldn't be deluded. We always have a blind side which we can't see but others may. In the past, we used our delusions and rationalizations as defenses to protect us and make us more comfortable in a hostile world. Then the last thing we wanted was for someone to tell us the truth about ourselves, and we let others know in subtle or not so subtle ways that we didn't want to hear it. Now, understanding that our delusions and rationalizations are symptoms of character defects which separate us from the love of God, the Kingdom of Heaven is revealed in reality, and we actively seek out others who can speak the truth in love and help us see ourselves as we really are.

The process is still painful and frightening. Remember, we claim progress, not perfection. Pride is alive, sleeping in a corner of our hearts, although this cell is continually narrowing, growing smaller and smaller. Pride still wants us to avoid the truth, saying we don't need to, we dare not look at this or that reality. Trust, experience and discipline keep us from running away. Experience shows us that discovering the worst aspects of our character defects isn't nearly as frightening or as damaging as our denial and delusions were in the past. The skeletons in our closets, seen in the light, aren't nearly as scary as we imagined, and denial and delusions kept us unable to love.

Having the benefit of the insight of others helps us see that we have made progress. If we become discouraged, our friend and sponsor reminds us of how far we've come. Our idea that we should be perfect is slow to go, and we often need to be reminded that progress, not perfection, is what we seek.

Often upon entering the program, many of us imagine that we can jump from Step One to Step Twelve without doing the intervening work. This is called "two-stepping," and is common among newcomers. Our partners can slow us down and help us realize that we won't approach perfection over-night. Sponsors remind us it took years for us to become the way we are, and we will continue progress in the steps the rest of our lives.

Our partners in progress can share our joy when we deepen our trust and experience of the love of God. Do you remember how happy you were the first time you fell in love? You wanted to tell every-one. When you did, your friends may have said something like, "You're in love with *him*?" not understanding your joy or what you saw in the beloved. The same is true with your experience of the love of God. In a sense, only those who have taken these steps or made spiritual progress through another route will understand your joy, and it is with these people that you will feel most at home.

This doesn't mean you won't share your joy with others. You will, but in the beginning you will do so less directly. Here is another snare our remaining pride will try to use to trap us—spiritual elitism. Even though we have a direct relationship with him, God doesn't love us any more than he loves anyone else. He loved us just as much when we were separated and lost. Remember the stories in Luke 15:1-10 of the lost coin and the lost sheep. To God, the lost coin is just as important as the one in his pocket; the lost sheep just as loved as those in the pen. Any tendency to look down on others who haven't taken the steps or had a spiritual awakening is contrary to God's will—God's will is only and always for us to be like him—unconditionally loving. Pride wants conditions, wants to be better than, wants to justify itself, hates to be the grateful recipient of God's grace. Most of us fall into this trap from time to time; our sponsors may help us notice it and climb out. The way is narrow, and only the grace of God, our continuous openness and willingness, and the help of others can keep us moving forward.

A sure sign of humility is recognition that we need help in developing the honesty required to work these steps. Another sure sign is our asking another person to join us in working the steps or, if the person has already begun the walk, to be our sponsor or spiritual leader. Asking another to be with us in our journey, we admit that our own approach to life was flawed and caused us pain; we weren't perfect! This is the first sacrament of a twelve-step program, the outward sign of an inward and spiritual grace, the grace of humility.

Deciding to invite others to be co-walkers or sponsors isn't as complicated as deciding with whom to share the fifth step. In a sense, almost anyone willing will do. Even a person who seems not to have made as much spiritual progress as we have is often able to see through our rationalizations. While we may not possess much insight into ourselves, often we can see through others very well. Also, we can have multiple co-walkers and sponsors. I always recommend and have at least two sponsors. This is not to get a variety of opinions so as to select the one most compatible with my own, but to make sure that at least one person is always available. If I ever ask for two opinions, I can be sure I'm looking for my own answer.

I've often heard people say they wanted a sponsor whose experiences matched their own so they could be more fully understood. Often this means they want a sponsor whose delusions match their own, who shares their distorted world-view, and who will help them rationalize and support their defenses. This will be of no help to them at all. We need co-walkers who are different from ourselves, but who share our desire to make spiritual progress through the steps. When I first came into A.A., I sought a sponsor who was educated and bright; a professional person. As I made progress, I realized that the persons I needed were those who had attained serenity, peace of mind and the freedom and happiness of promises. Sometimes, these people had the least formal education and financial resources.

If you have no opportunity to find a sponsor or spiritual leader who has experience with the steps, I encourage you to invite people who are different rather than like you to join you in your journey. In this way you can help them penetrate their delusions and they can help you see yours.

The main thing is to find a partner and begin. Don't get bogged down in details. Anyone will do, and you can gather others as you go. Once again, "easy does it, but darn it, do it." Enjoy yourself and each other, and enjoy the walk. Always, always remember, nothing is serious except the fact that nothing can separate you from the love of God.

Summary

Step One — *We admitted we were powerless over [fill in the blank], that our lives had become unmanageable.*

The admission of powerlessness comes with a price; the price is our pride. We will go on, sometimes endlessly, trying to control the things that are troubling in our lives. Usually we blame people, places and things, and exert ourselves mightily trying to change them to meet our needs. Unhappily, no matter how much willpower we throw at these things they do not satisfy our desires. We try changing them altogether—geographic cures, divorces, job moves—yet our distress follows us. Working Step One interrupts this endless struggle; we acknowledge powerlessness.

This step has two-parts; we acknowledge both powerlessness and unmanageability, although in a sense one is an extension of the other. We can sometimes admit powerlessness, but deny that we're affected by it. For instance, I'm powerless over anger, depression, anxiety, my child, food, my boss, my spouse, my finances, etc., but I don't let it bother me and I go on with my life. Once we acknowledge that the pain cripples us, and that powerlessness is, by definition, unmanageability, we can quit attempting to control the uncontrollable. Pride has made us unwilling to admit complete defeat, but humility is the key to opening ourselves to receive the power of God's love.

Step Two — *Came to believe that a Power greater than ourselves could restore us to sanity.*

Step One without a mind open to belief in a higher power would lead to despair. Looking honestly at the unmanageability of our lives, we would cry out, "Now what will you tell me? You've shattered my delusions of control and brought me to look honestly at the pain over which I'm powerless. You've left me undefended in a hopeless situation. You want to talk about God, but perhaps I don't believe in God. Perhaps I don't trust the God I've been taught to believe in. Perhaps I feel I'm not worthy of God's help." We begin to realize the twelve-step program brings results, miraculous results. We're told all we need is an open mind, to exchange doubt and disbelief for openness. Pride of intellect, pride of defiance and pride of thinking of ourselves as extra-specially bad persons can all be over come and belief can come through the simple process of opening the mind. We discover that either in or out of prayer we have always sought our own will, and have never unconditionally said, "Thy will be done."

Step Three — *Made a decision to turn our will and our lives over to the care of God as we understood Him.*

"Nothing's changed, but everything's different." This is an expression that describes the experience of making the decision contained in Step Three. The decision is a spiritual action wherein, having come to believe in a living, loving God with whom we can be in relationship, and whose power is greater than ours, we finally gave up our own unhappy struggle to run the show for ourselves and others, turning over our whole selves—physical, intellectual, emotional, and spiritual—to the God of our understanding. It is only to the "God of our understanding" that we become willing to turn because this represents God's nature revealed personally to us. It is only the God we understand that we can trust and believe to this degree.

Step Four — *Made a searching and fearless moral inventory of ourselves.*

Step Four can be attempted only after taking Steps Two and Three. We become able to take a "searching and fearless moral inventory of ourselves" only after we've turned our lives over to a loving, powerful God we can trust. Until now, we made searching, moral inventories of others, but when the searchlight was turned on us we rationalized, minimized, and blamed people, places and things for our shortcomings. In Step Four for the first time we eliminate blame from our spiritual vocabulary and accept responsibility for our character defects. This step is a giant step towards honesty and humility. Unless we recognize our character defects and take responsibility for them we can make no further spiritual progress.

We are surprised to discover that the sources of our emotional insecurities—worry, anger, self-pity and depression—are our own character defects rather than the fault of other people, places, and things. We find that our own defenses ambush us spiritually and emotionally. We have met the enemy, and it is us. The rewards for a thorough Step Four are new understanding and confidence, and rightened relationships. As we stop blaming others and take responsibility for our own defensiveness, our relationships improve.

Step Five — *Admitted to God, to ourselves, and to another human being the exact nature of our wrongs.*

Step Five is one of the three most difficult steps, and so one of the most freeing. This twelve-step pathway leads continually toward greater humility, which opens us increasingly to God's grace. Both the church and secular society understand the need for and benefits of confession, either through a priest, psychiatrist, counselor or friend. We are only as sick as our secrets. Without admitting our *worst* character defects to another person, we can *never* receive the peace of mind the steps promise. Careful choice of the person in whom to confide is important. The benefits of the step are as marvelous as the taking of it is terror-filled. They include becoming able to accept and to give forgiveness, a feeling of kinship with humanity, heightened honesty, tranquility, and oneness with God.

Step Six — *Were entirely ready to have God remove all these defects of character.*

In Step Six we grow in our awareness that our character defects, our defenses, are the source of all our difficulties. We more profoundly understand that it isn't what others do which disturbs us, it is our own fear that our needs won't be met which is the source of our emotional distress. We are angry, worried, and depressed because of our fear that we won't get our needs met—physical, emotional and ego-validating (need for self-esteem) or that we will lose something we have. This is why we violated our values through dishonest people-pleasing. Now we have turned our lives over to a powerful, loving God, from whom we get our validation. Since our defenses have become superfluous, we are entirely ready to have God remove them. With Step Two we begin a lifelong process that is never completed; thus the image of a circular stair on which we always come back to Step One, yet continue to make spiritual progress. The more we root out our defeating defenses and trust God, the freer we become and the more peace and joy we experience.

Step Seven — *Humbly asked Him to remove our shortcomings.*

As we make spiritual progress through believing and trusting God and taking responsibility for our fears, we discover that we are also powerless over our character defects and need God's help to remove them. We begin to understand on a more profound level that it is entirely in God that we "live, and move, and have our being," and that without him we can do nothing at all. It is from God that we get our physical strength, our capacity to feel and think, to work and play and all our other opportunities. We see that not only did we not write, produce, or direct life's play; we didn't even buy a ticket! So, because we love ourselves, we humbly ask him to remove our defects and defenses. In Step Seven we move even more out of ourselves and toward God.

Step Eight — *Made a list of all persons we had harmed, and became willing to make amends to them all.*

The goal of the following two steps is, "in light of the newfound knowledge of ourselves," to develop the best possible relationship with every human being we know.

This is another step that we never really finish, but it is vitally important for our spiritual growth and peace of mind to begin. Remember, we only make the list and *become willing*. We are not yet ready to make amends.

Step Eight is a three-part step, and the second part can't be well begun until the first part is underway. We may become embarrassed if we attempt to make amends when not spiritually mature enough to do so. Yet again, "easy does it, but darn it, do it!"

The first part of Step Eight has to do with forgiveness. Often the people we've harmed are those we feel have harmed us, and we can't consider asking their forgiveness until we have first forgiven them. We realize that we have been dealing with fellow sufferers who have acted out of fear and emotional emptiness and that our mutual defenses have fed each other's distress. Having done a thorough Step Four, we are no longer self-righteous; we understand that "there is none righteous, no, not one."

The second part includes defining "harm." Harm done to others includes the physical, mental, emotional, and/or spiritual damage we have done, and involves "sins" of omission as well as commission. A rule of thumb is that anyone with whom we have been angry we have probably harmed; anyone we don't want to see or talk to we have probably harmed. In the story of the prodigal son the father's running out to meet the son when he was far off (before he had apologized) showed not only his forgiveness of the son, but also the father's innocence toward the son.

The third part of the step is willingness. We must become willing to make amends.

The benefits include greater peace, partnership and fellowship with men and women and with God.

Step Nine — *Made direct amends to such people wherever possible, except when to do so would injure them or others.*

This is the second of the three hardest steps. Most other steps are done inwardly, and we can sometimes fool ourselves into believing that we've done them. This is another sacramental action step which involves others witnessing the reality of our humility.

Pride invites us to become confused over the words, "except when to do so would injure them or others." Often in meetings I've heard, "I'm one of the others not to be hurt in taking the ninth step." Often this signals fear and/or unwillingness to make the amends. It must be only out of love that we make the decision not to make amends, not for selfish reasons. We make the amends, not the offended person, and while it is a happy thing if the one offended accepts our amends, it is not required. What is important is that we open ourselves, not that the gesture is returned.

If amends are not made in a timely fashion, we make no further spiritual progress. This step demonstrates our willingness to take responsibility for our actions, to trust God to provide the resources, spiritual, emotional and physical to make the amends. It is the most significant sign of our spiritual development—the willingness to take responsibility for the well-being of others. The promises are coming true for us—self-seeking is slipping away, and we're experiencing true peace of mind.

Step Ten — *Continued to take personal inventory and when we were wrong promptly admitted it.*

The goal of all these steps is increased humility, making room for God's grace to enter us more fully, increasing his peace and power in our lives. Humility isn't degrading, it is an honest and realistic view of ourselves in relation to God and our place in creation. In our old, defensive mode, we pursued perfection and believed others expected it from us. We admitted only the faults or errors we thought were trivial, so we wouldn't appear arrogant. We burned with shame and anger if we were caught in an important mistake, and denied, blamed and rationalized it in an attempt to defend ourselves. Now that we know we have God's love and that he counts us righteous through his own will and action and not through our efforts, we can recognize our mistakes on a daily basis and make prompt amends when we harm others.

In taking our daily inventory, there will be things we have done well. We will see and feel God's grace in our hearts and lives. We will have held our tongue when we wanted to gossip. We will have had the grace to give someone a real compliment. We will have enjoyed playing with our children or listening to our spouse's conversation. We will move through tolerance and acceptance, and into true love for our neighbors—whoever is nearby.

Step Eleven — *Sought through prayer and meditation to improve our conscious contact with God as we understood Him, praying only for knowledge of His will and the power to carry that out.*

The amazing implication of Step Eleven: God is alive and we can have a personal relationship with him. We began and increased this relationship throughout the steps. As our awareness of God's grace grows, our desire for a more direct relationship increases. We find that prayer and meditation clear out the noise in our minds and souls to make a more direct relationship possible.

Through our pursuit of the steps, we discovered God knows all about us, but we knew little about him. Our parents may have told us things, or perhaps we had heard about God in church, and maybe we had read some things but, like Job, in the past we had only heard, now we KNOW. Now we have a direct relationship with God as a result of humbling ourselves, opening our minds, and accepting his will for us. We do not get into theological arguments with anyone.

Yet, since we are still fallible and willful people, (we claim progress, not perfection), we need anchors to keep us from floating adrift and following "other voices." Self-will often dresses up as the "still, small voice." Such meditative anchors include St. Francis's prayer, the Sermon on the Mount, the Summary of the Law, and the Letter of James. There are forms of meditation that are less than helpful; we need to be sure whose spirit we are inviting in!

We pray only for knowledge of God's will and the power to carry it out. In the past we scarcely knew what was good for us; now we find we pray less often for specifics for ourselves or others. Through our experience of God's increasing grace in our lives we have learned to trust that all things work together for good for those who love him, and that he is the best judge of what is good for us.

Step Twelve — *Having had a spiritual awakening as the result of these steps, we tried to carry this message to others, and to practice these principles in all our affairs.*

Here are some of Bill W.'s words about the twelfth step: "When a man or woman has a spiritual awakening, the most important meaning of it is that he has now become able to do, feel and believe that which he could not do before on his unaided strength and resources alone…. He has been set on a path which tells him he is really going somewhere, that life is not a dead end, not something to be endured or mastered. In a very real sense he has been transformed because he has laid hold of a source of strength which, in one way or another, he had hitherto denied himself. He finds himself in possession of a degree of honesty, tolerance, unselfishness, peace of mind, and love of which he had thought himself quite incapable."

These are qualities that can't be hidden. And they are very attractive! People will want what you have. You will carry the message in your living as well as in your conversation, as you practice these principles. There will be many who think the program is foolishness, that you just don't understand the real world. How deluded they are, just as you were! These steps aren't for everyone who needs them, but for anyone who wants them. There will be those who want them.

As we practice these principles, we continually come back to the first step and repeat the cycle with more profound openness, understanding and a deeper willingness to receive God's grace.

Anger — What is it and why, contrary to present popular belief, is it spiritually wrong? The founders of Christianity were correct in considering anger a deadly sin. It kills both body and the soul. An angry person is a fearful person, not trusting that God can, will and does meet all his needs. Anger is physically destructive, causing stress, lowered immune response and cardiovascular problems. Anger causes mental confusion and impairs our judgment. In battle or in a sports match, we're told to "keep a cool head" because anger is defeating. It is deadly to deny and repress anger, but there is a spiritual alternative to anger and the expression of anger: "The *Lord* is my refuge and my *sure defense*." When we trust God there is no need for anger. As the "Big Book," *Alcoholics Anonymous*, says, "We believe God is sovereign and nothing happens which he doesn't allow and which

157

he will not ultimately work out for our good."

To Work — One of the first signs of humility, the quality we pursue, is recognition that we need help in developing the honesty required to work these steps. Working them with others—at least one other—is far preferable to working them alone. *These steps should not be worked with family members or people with whom we have an inter-dependent relationship.*

Find a partner who doesn't share your character defects, someone who will help you see through your delusions. Do not pick someone you feel you relate to closely; rather pick someone whose experiences are different and who has a different point of view. This will foster humility and spiritual growth for both or all of you.

The promises always come true for those willing to work them.

Alcoholics Anonymous, A.A. World Services, Inc. 1976, p. 103.